on track ...
Suzanne Vega

Lisa Torem

SONICBOND

sonicbondpublishing.com

Sonicbond Publishing Limited
www.sonicbondpublishing.co.uk
Email: info@sonicbondpublishing.co.uk

First Published in the United Kingdom 2023
First Published in the United States 2023

British Library Cataloguing in Publication Data:
A Catalogue record for this book is available from the British Library

Copyright Lisa Torem 2023

ISBN 978-1-78952-281-5

Typeset in ITC Garamond Std & ITC Avant Garde Gothic Pro
Printed and bound in England
Graphic design and typesetting: Full Moon Media

Follow us on social media:
Twitter: https://twitter.com/SonicbondP
Instagram: https://www.instagram.com/sonicbondpublishing_/
Facebook: https://www.facebook.com/SonicbondPublishing/

Linktree QR code:

on track ...
Suzanne Vega

Contents

Acknowledgements

The following individuals contributed greatly to this project: musician Ian Anderson, producer Steve Addabbo, producer/performer Richard Barone, Joel Cohen, CEO Martin Goldschmidt, guitarist Jonathan Gordon, singer-songwriters Lucille Kaplansky and Jann Klose, Anne Leighton, producer Gerry Leonard, photographer Philamonjaro, filmmaker Christopher Seufert, composer Duncan Sheik, composer/arranger John Philip Shenale, creative consultants Emily Torem, Madeline Torem, readers John Clarkson and Christopher Torem and author Robbie Woliver.

CHICAGO, IL

SV - ▬▬▬▬▬▬▬

MARLENA	2
FREEZE TAG	-
CARAMEL	-
GYPSY	2
IN LIVERPOOL	8
QUEEN AND THE SOLDIER	2
FRANK AND AVA	2
NY IS MY DESTINATION	-
HARPER LEE	-
NY IS WOMAN	-
LEFT OF CENTER	-
I NEVER WEAR WHITE	-
SOME JOURNEY	O
LUKA	2
TOM'S DINER	-

* *

DREAMING (BLONDIE)	-
TOMBSTONE	-
ROSEMARY	2

Above: Vega's February 2023 setlist from Chicago's Old Town School of Folk Music included studio career highlights. (*Lisa Torem*)

Introduction

Writing in other voices is almost Japanese in the sense that there's a certain
formality there which allows me to sidestep the embarrassment of directly
expressing to complete strangers the most intimate details of my life.
**Suzanne Vega to Mark Woodworth in 1998 for *Solo: Women Singer-
songwriters in Their Words*.**

In multiple interviews, the award-winning recording artist clarified that she
did not initially write songs with the purpose of achieving commercial gain;
her trajectory was seemingly more about discovering her voice as a poet and
a storyteller, yet success came along just the same.

In 1987, Vega garnered a Grammy for 'Best Female Pop Vocal Performer'
for 'Luka'. Four singles: 'Marlene on the Wall,' 'Left of Center,' 'Luka' and 'No
Cheap Thrill' saturated the Top 40 charts in the UK in the 1980s and 1990s.
With her team, Vega also won awards designated by *Billboard*, *Zebrik*,
Glamour, *Peabody*, *Drama Desk*, *NME*, *ASCAP*, *Pollstar* and *MTV*.

On the original version of 'Tom's Diner' from 1987 sophomore album,
Solitude Standing, Vega rendered the song a cappella, but in 1990, the
British duo DNA remixed the track, featuring Vega as lead soloist. In
this unexpected incarnation, 'Tom's Diner' claimed a Top 10 position in
multiple countries, including Germany, Greece and Switzerland. *99.9.F* was
proclaimed 'Best Rock Album' in 1993 by New York Music Awards. In 2008,
Beauty & Crime was voted 'Best Engineered Album, Non-Classical' by the
Recording Academy.

Yet at the core, none of that success, incidental or not, appears to have
altered Vega's principles, along her 40-year path. Rather than follow the
latest trend, she has vigilantly upheld the sacred craft of storytelling, joining
the ranks of screenwriters and novelists, who have created and developed
timeless characters.

Furthermore, she has intelligently bridged the gap between artist and
audience; Vega and her fans are strongly connected. I see her transparency
as a strong factor. We have seen our loneliest, scariest and proudest selves in
her bodies of work. There are the intrepid characters that we might love or
befriend if given the chance, but even the protagonists that teeter on the edge
give purpose to her narratives.

Vega has been compared to Bob Dylan, lyrically, but she in turn, has
influenced a variety of successful singer-songwriters (some of whom I will
cover), as well. Whether choosing to present material in a contemporary
folk, neo-folk or techno-folk fashion, she has fearlessly bucked trends. Some
songs rely on the strophic structure, while others are arranged in distinctive
sections, yet her often-idiomatic intent consistently shines through. In all
aspects, she expresses a voice uniquely her own.

In an interview with the author on 19 June 2015, Vega discussed finding her
niche while expanding her thematic range:

I came down to The Village with the idea of playing Gerdes Folk City, where Bob Dylan had gotten his start, and I came down there with my acoustic guitar. So, in some ways, I am a folkie in that old-fashioned sense of standing on stage with my guitar and telling stories and all that.

But even from the very beginning, I had never let that define me or limit me, so that's why I was able to write a song like 'Cracking' because I thought, 'let's do this.' I was influenced by the rock music that I was listening to, by Lou Reed, by New Wave artists and, by some degree, the punks, although I don't shout or scream, but there is a bit of a punk influence in there as well as a minimalist kind of aesthetic. So, I let that all seep in, which is what I think you're supposed to do if you want to be an artist.

She was born in Santa Monica, California to her British biological father, Richard Peck, and biological mother, Pat Schumacher, a German-Swedish computer systems analyst. After their divorce, her family moved to 'Spanish Harlem' and the Upper West Side of New York City.

Her mother remarried. Vega's stepfather, Edgardo Vega Yunque, also known by his pen name, Ed Vega, was a Puerto Rican novelist and short story writer, whose works include the novel, *The Comeback*, and short stories 'Mendoza's Dreams' and 'Casualty Report'. He was inspired by William Faulkner, John Steinbeck and Ernest Hemingway.

She was the oldest of four children, which also included Tim, Alyson and Matthew Vega. In interviews, she admits that she was a late talker. She didn't mirror the typical toddler by pointing to an object and blurting out 'pie' or 'plane.'

According to her stepfather, when she finally spoke, she didn't use monosyllabic shout-outs – she spoke in metaphors. It was as though she'd made a conscious choice to take note of sights and sounds and wait for the proper moment to share her visions with the world.

That world was colorful, often chaotic and inspirational. To host Kevin Burke on the podcast *Your Hometown Virtual Conversation* with Suzanne Vega on 22 June 2021, the songwriter discussed a factor that strongly influenced her writing – the multi-culturalism she experienced growing up in New York City proper:

I can't imagine how I'd have written if I had come from a town where everyone was the same demographic; my mother came from the Midwest, and so therefore, it was more of a similar demographic. But in my neighborhoods, it was wildly diverse. In East Harlem, we had mixtures of black, Puerto Rican, Irish. On the upper west side, we had Europeans. We had different ages and every type of point-of-view you could imagine. So, that was important to me, growing up.

She also commented on the art, sculpture, poetry workshops and theater available mere steps away. These artistic happenings fueled her imagination, made her curious about others and contributed to an overall sense of artistic freedom.

Vega has consistently been a keen observer of human behavior. Her 2001 book, *The Passionate Eye: The Collected Writing of Suzanne Vega*, includes stories, poems and lyrics that only an acutely self-aware individual could create. Although much of the writings originated in her early teens, a handful of early works include a haiku written at age eleven and a poem, *By Myself*, written at age nine (the same age in which she discovered that Ed Vega was not her biological father).

Despite age discrepancies, a common denominator weaves through these writings, irrespective of the formats. Each lyric, story and poem provide clues to Vega's 'outsider' perspectives and illustrate her innate hunger for self-expression.

In the story, 'The Piano,' for instance, written at age fifteen, Vega zeroes in on the disciplined lives of young dancers. Through dialogue and narrative, she makes us painfully aware of how frequently body imagery judgments come into play in the realm of the performing arts.

In reality, she learned to feel comfortable expressing herself as a dancer, but later, as a guitar-playing performer, she found it challenging to move freely on stage while strumming an instrument or being responsible for switching chord shapes while accompanying herself.

Years later, when Vega performs live, she shows no signs of putting either herself or her audience on a pedestal but has acknowledged in interviews that she is aware of being watched and even scrutinized. She understands that her movements and manner of speaking matter. She strives to communicate through her poetic lyrics and melodies, but she regards herself, and the audience, as separate entities.

Many stories reflected slices of authentic life. Vega was a dance major at New York's highly competitive Fiorello H. LaGuardia High School of Music and Art and Performing Arts, which loosely provided the dramatic inspiration for the 1980 American film, *Fame*. This rigorous high school closed in 1984 and included alumni such as Liza Minelli and Eartha Kit, among others.

Vega then attended Barnard College, an all-women school situated across from Columbia University in Morningside Heights, where she graduated with a degree in English, while concurrently expanding her interest in music. In fact, what had attracted her to the discipline of dance in the first place was actually the music; the wildfire behind the beats.

It was a busy four years. She worked concurrently as a receptionist and graduated with the Class of 1982. The Mortarboard Yearbook from the *digitalcollections.barnard.edu* of 1981 reveals a black-and-white image of a serious student with then-shoulder-length hair.

Vega returned with musician Laurie Anderson, Class of 1969, and comedian Joan Rivers, Class of 1954, for the 'Barnard Performs' benefit at Carnegie Hall in commemoration of their centennial on 8 February 1989. In another archival photo, Vega stands at the end of a lineup applauding; she's dressed in a tailored dress, dark tights and stylish black boots.

For her undergraduate thesis, she combined her passion for literature and music by composing several songs inspired by Southern author Carson McCullers'ss short stories which she developed into an original one-act play. This admiration for McCullers's body of work never waned, and Vega later, as shall be seen, developed the project with award-winning American songwriter and composer Duncan Sheik. Their collaboration, *Carson McCullers Talks About Love*, appeared off-Broadway in 2011 at Rattlestick Theater, a company known for promoting new playwrights.

Her neighborhood has played a distinctive role in Vega's lyrics. Barnard College is walking distance to 112th and Broadway, the bustling intersection which houses Tom's Restaurant, a place that Americans might describe as a typical 'greasy spoon,' rife with comfort food and bottomless cups of coffee. Barnard is merely a brisk jaunt, too, from the landmark-status John the Divine Church: both buildings are immortalized in 'Tom's Diner.'

Vega had the talent to be successful in a number of disciplines but music, and more specifically, songwriting, trumped other disciplines by the end of her scholarly stint.

The first incarnation of Gerdes Folk City on 11 W. 4th in New York City's legendary Greenwich Village functioned as an Italian restaurant. Owned by proprietor Mike Porco, the original locale featured incidental music prior to concentrating on live acts. In its prime, the likes of Judy Collins, Joan Baez, Pete Seeger, Emmylou Harris and Bob Dylan enjoyed the flexibility and freedom of testing out original material at Gerdes. Although a humble place in the physical sense, the club achieved major acclaim.

According to *The Rolling Stones Book of Lists*, Gerdes' legacy ran parallel to that of The Cavern Club, the Mathew Street venue in Liverpool, England, where The Beatles wooed screaming girls in the 1960s, and CBGB's, a grittier village outpost, where coarse graffiti sectioned off bathroom stalls; The Patti Smith Group, The Ramones, Blondie, Television and Talking Heads held court there as new wave and punk spread its furious seed. During Gerdes' heyday in the 1970s, Vega performed at their latter location (130 W. 3rd); the ambience provided a welcoming oasis for her and other success-driven innovators.

Gerdes had not been Vega's first or only choice for being seen and heard, but when the ambitious teen made the rounds with her acoustic guitar, she got turned down at The Other End – aka The Bitter End. Nevertheless, she forged on unfazed. After all, it was nothing personal. The Bitter End proprietors were interested in promoting established acts. That being said, Vega shifted gears and approached venues that genuinely held promise for acts hawking original songs.

The modestly staged club was a reliable fit. Vega could usually get a hold of a bass player, but she was essentially a self-contained, female act.

Since Gerdes offered the chance to cultivate a steady clientele, the physical environment may have been of secondary concern.

Cold calling took gumption, but Vega prepared herself by doing research. Gerdes' attendees were of the open-minded variety. Even if the management hadn't taken stock of Vega, she'd studied their cultural history. Vega explained to *The New York Times* on 13 September 1985:

> I was drawn to Folk City after reading Bob Dylan's biography, which I knew backward and forward. I dreamed that if I could just get a gig there, I would have it made, but it took me several years to work up the courage to actually go inside.

New York natives can often distinguish among cultural enclaves. But while the West Village ambience varied from street to street, overall, it was a hotspot for entertainers and tourists alike.

Gerdes doubled as a magnet for the talent only steps away on McDougal Street at the Speakeasy, home of the Fast Folk Cooperative. Rod McDonald, a prominent member, who lived across the street, chronicled ideologies of the time: 'Man with a Hired Face' was a protest song, for instance, about then-American president Ronald Reagan.

McDonald and friends commonly wrote about other burning issues facing their community: home insecurity, substance abuse and corporate America. As such, folksingers that gigged at both venues, irrespective of any professional competition, created a collective energy and a receptive fanbase.

Vega also frequented the singular-roomed Cornelia Street Café (considered one of the best overall clubs in which to hear jazz). It opened in 1977 but became one more casualty of escalating rents and is now defunct.

Jack Hardy, an influential, early mentor, founded the Songwriter's Exchange, the Speakeasy Museum's Co-op, and the *Fast Folk Musical Magazine* (a combination record album and magazine) and served as the label owner of Great Divide Records. The Boston Globe cited Hardy as 'one of the most influential figures in defining the American folk song.'

Vega attended Monday night songwriting circles hosted at his Houston Street dwelling. Over steaming pasta and copious bottles of wine, a cluster of hopefuls received critiques from Hardy and peers. The dining approach and revolving influx of artists suggest a laid-back vibe, but Hardy commanded a tight ship: memorized arrangements were subject to serious analysis.

In an excerpt from *Some Journey*, a still-in-progress documentary by Christopher Seufert, Vega fumbled for bills in a yellow taxi near her mentor's Greenwich Village apartment; her nerves were on edge at the thought of performing before cerebral songwriters and Hardy. Despite having achieved a high level of success with her music, since the early Village days, she was visibly nervous. After all, Hardy would still hold Vega to his exemplary standards.

Having survived the experience, Vega shared this appraisal: 'I really liked what I was hearing and I liked the quality of the songwriting that was happening. It was kind of like a good platform to just start coming in with little sketches again.' She described the comfortably attired attendees as 'a very loose group of people who like to drink a lot and discuss songwriting.'

On 'The Boulevardiers' from her 1985 self-titled debut, Vega paid tribute to those tense but creatively fulfilling days. When listening to Hardy's music, it's easy to understand Vega's deep admiration.

His melodic, finger-style introductions, mythological imagery, Celtic-inspired themes and political overtones captivate. And as mentioned earlier, when Vega performed in front of the crowded room, she was given no free pass despite her show business status. Hardy looked her squarely in the eyes when giving feedback: Had she thought enough about the melody?

In an interview with Hardy in 2000, printed on *www.jackhardy.com*, Vega queried him about his philosophy, specifically: 'that the song is more important than the singer and that's what creates a folk song.' Hardy responded with: '...if the song is any good, it means that a hundred years from now they'll still be singing it, long after they've forgotten who wrote it.' She also asked how much of his material was autobiographical; did he have other 'rules of thumb?' Hardy replied: 'Even if you're observing what someone else is doing, you're the one who's chosen to pick that to observe.'

He stressed that the relationship between artist and audience is a 'two-way street,' and despaired that 'a lot of modern songwriters, they're writing it just for what they want to express or it's all about them.'

When examining Hardy's role as an early songwriting mentor, one can draw parallels between his no-nonsense philosophies and Vega's own holistic approach to performance. While some performers accumulate their 10,000 hours through trial and error, Vega, even at the early stages of her career, seemed more prone to use her 'third eye,' which *dictionary.com* describes as: 'an inner vision and enlightenment beyond what the physical eyes can see' and which 'provides perception beyond ordinary insight.' She learned from those in her inner circle as well as talented predecessors.

In 1978, Robbie Woliver, Marilyn Lash and Joseph Hillesum took over booking and eventually purchased Gerdes in 1980. But economics was not on their side. Rapidly rising rents and insurmountable soundproofing issues warranted a move to the East Village; the new locale guaranteed a 400-seat capacity.

While the move made sense monetarily, the feelings of dyed-in-the-wool performers sometimes bubbled to the surface. Singer-songwriter Lucille Kaplansky, for *The New York Times* article, 'Folk City Ends 25-Year West Village Stand,' 28 March 1986, lamented: 'The East Village is different, the people are different. It's just too sad to stand here and think about saying goodbye to your home.'

Despite the East versus West Village conundrum, communities stuck together. Meanwhile, the co-owners took note of incoming trends and expanded the scope of acceptable acts. These polished acts paved the way for a spectrum of alternative pioneers. Bob Dylan, Odetta, Joan Baez, John Lee Hooker, Peter, Paul and Mary and Pete Seeger had primed the cultural pump, but Vega and peers became key purveyors of an unexpected revolution: a distinguished 'second wave' of singer-songwriters (Woliver kept history alive by authoring *Bringing It All Back Home: 25 Years of American Music at Folk City* in 1986, retitled as *Hoot! A Twenty-Five Year History Of The Greenwich Village Music Scene* in the 1990s. Woliver also immortalized the club with the musical, *Folk City*, produced at Theater for the New City in New York City and the Brunish Theater in Portland, Oregon in 2018).

Vega, who made fast friends, regarded her contemporaries in the Village scene as 'a supportive group of fellow musicians and curious onlookers.' For all intents and purposes, Elvis Costello, 10,000 Maniacs, Richard Thompson and Sonic Youth set the tone for an innovative brand of 1980s music; a vital part of a burgeoning scene, they sustained this alt-revival.

There was more room at the top for female artists, too. Critics began to appreciate individual differences, whereas prior to that time, the soft-spoken Vega might have been twinned with husky-voiced 10,000 Maniac's vocalist Natalie Merchant.

Yet the artists faced challenges; an inner divide was brewing between the classicists and 'left of center' artists. Singer-songwriters that borrowed acoustic strumming, heartfelt vocals and socio-political themes vis a vis the sixties had to muscle their way into the shifting scene.

David Browne in 'How Bob Dylan's Rolling Thunder Revue Paved the Way for the Eighties Folk Revival,' 20 June 2019, claimed: '...most of these musicians were largely ignored, even by the local press,' whereas Sonic Youth and Swans lit up CBGB's and the Mudd Club.

To her credit, Vega was savvy enough to strike a balance between both worlds. Was that due to her bravado, timing or talent? In that same article, Browne rolled the dice on the latter variable: 'Recent Barnard graduate Suzanne Vega was writing and singing, brittle, beautiful affectless songs about relationships and states of mind.'

Mark Wayne Glasmire opened for Vega in 1985. In the article, 'L.V. Performers Land Slot for NYC Folk Club Celebration Entertainment' by Tim Blangger and The Morning Call, 13 September 1985, the singer-songwriter explains that he exhausted his gas tank budget for the chance to sing two songs, or whatever he could pack into an eight-minute spot per the open-mic policy.

When Glasmire saw Vega perform under red-hot lights, he shared early producer Steve Addabbo's reaction: 'She had tremendous stage presence. She was so confident. It was amazing.' Glasmire went on to win awards and garner international airplay.

The term 'neo-folk' describes a genre that fuses experimental folk with industrial music. Proponents often used apocalyptic themes to drive home perspectives.

Accordingly, songs that hinged on poetic realism hit the bullseye. One reviewer compared Vega's palpable prose to the work of Sylvia Plath, a poet who commonly laced dark imagery throughout her volumes of work.

Vega spoke of fragmented dreams and lives untethered and her audiences responded in kind. She, and her colleagues, may have stood on the shoulders of the beats and the flower children, as far as the popular press was concerned, but the beats and flower children had come and gone. in their place stood a more realistic crowd: 'If I walked into a folk club and came upon this woman strumming her songs, I'd be impressed too – she picks her words with evident care and *conversationalizes* her chosen vocal tradition with evident savvy,' critic R. Christgau wrote on 30 July 1985 in the *Village Voice*. Christgau's review brought curious crowds to Gerdes.

Vega keeps up ties. In 2010, well after Gerdes closed, Vega performed at a 50-year reunion held by Mike Porco's grandson, Bob Porco, who, like Woliver, stood determined to keep the club's history alive through word-of-mouth and documentation.

It is as important to understand Vega's influence as it is to understand the ways in which she has been influenced. One major influence was Lou Reed. In 1979, a friend invited Vega to her first rock concert featuring Reed. The progressive singer/songwriter/performer would likely have been promoting The Bells Tour at Columbia University or performing at the Ritz.

Vega arrived with no preconceived notions of Reed's solo music, having never heard of him, or his former iconic band, The Velvet Underground, although she was familiar with the song speech of 'Walk on the Wild Side.'

Vega's exposure to Reed instigated a cultural sea change. In her formative years, she'd been attentive, among other things, to the tastes of her guitar-playing stepfather. He'd been partial to rural-based fare, which may have included homespun story songs such as: 'If I Had a Hammer' co-written by Pete Seeger, or 'Goodnight Irene' and 'Rock Island Line' by twelve-string virtuoso Huddie William Ledbetter, AKA Lead Belly.

Such repertoire was flush with catchy lyrics and easy-to-imitate guitar licks, but were the themes enough to sustain Vega's interest during her college years? Exemplary train routes and metaphors about 'hammering out justice' had little to do with a fast-paced, urban existence, although she admired her predecessors greatly.

In contrast to these early folk heroes, Reed was a brooding raconteur. With his introspective originals, he frequently broached themes considered uncomfortably candid for the times. While 'Walk on the Wild Side' ironically represented the lighter portion of his set, 'Carolyn Says II' tells a story of abuse from a rare female standpoint. The ironic title 'Perfect Day' belied the suicidal theme. 'Coney Island Baby' included startling spoken word and electrified riffs. And Coney Island was an actual place that a mobile New Yorker could get to on public transportation, just a short stop away from Brighton Beach. These stories did not revolve around Depression-era hobos clinging to rickety freight trains or racehorses, like Lead Belly's lovable 'Stewball'.

In Lisa Robinson's *Here Comes Gravity, a Life in Rock and Roll*, the music journalist asked Reed about his motivation: Why did he pretend to shoot up during the song, 'Heroin'? Reed answered: 'If they want to see someone make believe he's shooting up and they get their rocks off at age 50, well, at that time of my life, I was happy to stand there like a ghoul and do it.'

Reed preferred playing smaller halls because: 'I hope the barbarians won't be there. I want the show to be for people who aren't interested in my pretending to shoot up during 'Heroin'.

It stands to reason, then, that Vega wrote the innocent ballads 'Gypsy' and 'Calypso' prior to witnessing Reed's raw iterations, and that 'Neighborhood Girls' and the aforementioned 'Cracking' were penned afterwards. These later songs toy with one's emotions, with tense words underlying the conversational tone.

Reed's set was rough-hewn but ultimately liberating. Vega didn't shun her folk roots thereafter, but she gave herself permission to embrace her own surroundings and tackle subjects that felt previously out-of-bounds or taboo, and she did so without apologies.

Reed's performance was hard-hitting. Vega pointed out a markedly visceral moment to *stevepafford.com* on the seventh anniversary of Reed's death: 'He was smoking, throwing lit cigarettes at the audience and miming shooting up onstage. It felt like that moment in *Taxi Driver* where he takes a woman to a porn film.' (Vega was referencing Travis Bickle, the Mohawked tough portrayed by Robert De Niro in the controversial 1976 American film).

Vega was no stranger to overt drug use, having witnessed substance abuse in the 1960s in Central Park and beyond, yet seeing an artist act out so provocatively as part of a paid performance was stunning.

This 'shock rock' approach may have been unnerving, but Vega's date explained that Reed's music was the genuine draw. In any event, Vega was sold. She purchased a couple of albums and became somewhat obsessed. Reed's images and insights often mirrored Vega's own observations about humanity or inhumanity: 'What I loved about Lou was his drive to tell the truth,' she told Evan Toth in September 2021 on YouTube.

Reed reframed Vega's worldview significantly. For example, the violence she'd become accustomed to on the streets, which could often be emotionally difficult to process, could legitimately find a pocket in this off-beat musical oeuvre. Reed also influenced Vega vocally; in future sets, she could be heard mimicking Reed's laid-back, you-are-there style.

But these discoveries didn't affect her loyalty to the already-established community. Vega still seemingly valued the folk and pop singers with whom she'd established a rapport. In fact, over the years, Vega has sustained friendships and professional relationships with other like-minded, urban singer-songwriters, especially those who thread physical place into the narrative.

Vega has opened for, among others, prog rock band Jethro Tull, whose multi-instrumentalist frontman, Ian Anderson, told the author in August 2022 that 'I love Suzanne Vega's music.' She has also performed alongside 'Walking to Nashville' writer Marc Cohn.

Producer, performer and author Richard Barone frequented the Greenwich Village circuit:

> My relationship started with Suzanne a long time ago. My first tour was when she was on an American tour in support of *Solitude Standing*. It was great because I was going on my first solo tour, which was separate from The Bongos. We became friends back then. It's through Pete Seeger, though, that we got to sing together. I think that's when we started playing at different events together. It was the George Wein (Newport Folk Fest founder) Tribute. Seeger played with us. What Suzanne represented to me, living in Greenwich Village, was the revitalization of the Village scene because it was an explosion of all of these artists, but then it went through a lull in terms of the popularity of the Village scene. But she was part of a resurgence of the mid-80s throughout the later part of the mid-80s, coming out of the Speakeasy, Gerdes Folk City and a few other venues where Suzanne would play. It was a new kind of freshness to the folk scene, a new kind of folk music. It was a more modern style and that was a big inspiration to me and a motivation for my solo work and in terms of my playing a little more acoustic music. It affected me for sure. .. We came way after the 1960s, but we knew about the 1960s. We both have that love about that era. She just performed with me Thursday night at the Museum of the City of New York. She sang a Velvet Underground song and I backed her up on acoustic guitar. We love Lou Reed and the Velvet Underground, but we connected that music to the Greenwich Village scene... I see Lou Reed in her music. It's not like an imitative thing, I see a brutal honesty. And there's this type of writing that she had done that is almost reportage, where she's reporting on things that happened on the streets or what happened in her neighborhood.

Vega was the support act for Leonard Cohen's 28-song set and triple encore set at Weybridge, Surrey, England at Mercedes-Benz World in 2009. Cohen and Vega developed a mutual respect, poetically and conversationally. She recorded an admirable cover of Cohen's 'Story of Isaac' for the *Tower of Song* tribute album and published an interview with the Canadian storyteller in *A Passionate Eye*.

Singer-songwriter-guitarist Jann Klose, another simpatico support act, who has lived in South Africa, Germany and cities in the US, currently resides in the New York borough of Queens. Like Vega, he approaches songwriting from a variety of contemporary angles but also treasures traditions. Klose, too, was exposed to the song stories of Pete Seeger and ventured into other genres, opening for Vega on 17 November 2017 in Sellersville, Pennsylvania.

In an interview with the author on 30 May 2022, Klose recalled his reaction to Vega's public persona and explained how he felt their storytelling strategies often aligned:

> I have always been a fan but seeing her live was quite enjoyable. She is one of those writers that surprises you with the unexpected. New York is always full of stories; there's never a lack of material. I think that probably informs my writing. I do a lot of traveling so that definitely plays into it as well.

Vega also partnered up for a title track with another kindred soul. In the article, 'Bill Morrissey, Blue-Collar Angst with a Folk Touch' by S. Holden, published on 23 February 1992 in *The New York Times*, Holden critiques Vega's participation in the folk singer's album, *Inside*:

> Singing in a quiet, gravelly voice against which Suzanne Vega's softer harmony rings like a mournful echo, Mr. Morrissey, a 40-year-old folk singer and songwriter from New England, describes the dreary existence of an unemployed worker who has recently given up drinking.

Singer-songwriter Lucille Kaplansky was greatly encouraged by Vega. Jeff Spevak wrote about Kaplansky and Vega in the article, 'Lucy Kaplansky's Songs Tell of her Journey' for *democratsandchronicle.com* on 21 September 2013: 'It was Suzanne Vega, already an established songwriter, who got Kaplansky thinking that she could get beyond singing other people's songs.' Kaplansky said: 'She heard this song I wrote when I was like, 20. She really liked this one line, the only good line: 'My mother told me to be a dark mystery, but that darkness is out of control.'

In an interview with the author on 30 August 2022, Kaplansky reiterated Vega's musical influence and further speculated on that line:

> That is a really old song of mine – I never perform it anymore – 'Only a Woman', which I wrote in about 1983. I guess, it was a pretty good line in a not-very-good song – that's why it stood out ... We met as students at Barnard College. Someone put us on a double bill (in a dorm) called 'Women in Music.' I remember being blown away by her. I specifically remember her singing 'Gypsy' and thinking it was fantastic. We became friends. I was already hanging out in the folk music scene in Greenwich Village, mostly at a place called Folk City (no longer there). Apparently, I told her to come down there with me, and I introduced her to everyone in the scene. We met in 1980 in Speakeasy, which opened in about 1982.

When asked if she went on to collaborate with other performers, Kaplansky replied: 'Lots! Shawn Colvin mostly: she showed up in 1980. I sang harmony with lots of people: Eric Andersen, Rod McDonald and Jim Dawson.' She graced the studio early in Vega's career: 'I sang on 'Left of Center', around 1984. The producer was Steve Addabbo. I came up with the harmony part with Steve's help.' Vega's repertoire had a lasting effect:

I've been inspired by many of her songs. 'Gypsy' and 'The Queen and the Soldier' both come to mind: partly melodically, but it's also the depth and beauty of the lyrics. I love her first and second albums. She was performing most of the songs on the first album when I met her.

Vega's interest in first folk wave singer-songwriter, Bob Dylan cannot be underestimated. For the article, 'Women on Bob Dylan' printed on 16 October 2016 in *The Observer* and *The Guardian*, Vega was one of six female songwriters asked to chime in on why the Minnesotan troubadour deserved to win the Nobel Prize for Literature in 2016 and to talk about his specific influence. She concurred:

Dylan was a big influence for me. He opened up the incredible, imaginary world. I was nine or ten when I first heard 'Mr. Tambourine Man' and I had a vision of him dancing 'beneath a diamond sky with one hand waving free.'

Material from *Days of Open Hand*, among others, mirrors Dylan's metaphorical proclivities. In that same article, Vega elaborates: 'I see a whole range of female characters in his music from goddesses and queens and women revered and then also women used, abused.'

Dylan, like Reed, wrote about issues that profoundly affected the well-being of women, and because female artists hadn't always had access to their own platform, their perspectives may have been especially validating – although Vega cited Lucinda Williams in the article, too, as well as other female artists in other outlets.

Perhaps Dylan even influenced the imagery and structure of 'The Queen and The Soldier'; he often favored the 'strophic' form, a popular songwriting style often used in the folk genre, whereby a single melodic and harmonic verse is repeated, but with varying lyrics.

He didn't invent this form. Like many songwriters, Dylan borrowed from early influences. Woody Guthrie used the strophic form in his famous 'talking songs', but this efficient system harkens back further to hymns and African-American spirituals, which Vega would also echo in future works, particularly with Duncan Sheik.

Dylan used the strophic structure to spin detailed narratives, such as 'Maggie's Farm', 'Don't Think Twice, It's Alright', 'Positively 4th Street' and

'Blowin' in the Wind', among others. The structural simplicity facilitates emboldened narratives sans harmonic disruption.

But Vega's songs can be compared to Dylan's in other ways: the mysterious descriptors of 'Small Blue Thing' shadow his ability to suggest a state of mind, yet not be wedded to it. Dylan refused to force-feed the listener by filling in all the blanks, and Vega follows suit. Both songwriters appear to take pride in holding something back; listeners get engaged in the dialogue in real time.

In an author interview on 13 March 2012, Vega said that she'd also been heavily influenced by singer-songwriter, pianist and fellow New Yorker Laura Nyro, specifically, her first three albums: 1967's *More Than a New Discovery*, 1968's *Eli and the Thirteenth Confession* and 1969's *New York Tendaberry*.

Nyro scored hits for 'Blood Sweat and Tears', 'Barbra Streisand', 'Three Dog Night', 'The Fifth Dimension' and 'Peter Paul and Mary', among others. She unabashedly broke standard harmonic rules with her atypical, dissonant chordal structures, and she experimented intrepidly with meter, not unlike bebop jazz musicians of the American jazz scene.

She liberally used poetic devices in her lyrics and titles. If the younger version of Suzanne Vega required a fountainhead, the three-octave-voiced Nyro was an excellent choice.

Vega paid it forward when she participated in the 2005 BBC Radio 2 documentary, *Shooting Star – Laura Nyro Remembered*, which was narrated by Bette Midler and included songs by Janis Ian, an alumni of Vega's inner-city high school.

But it was not only Nyro as the songwriter that intrigued Vega; she was also struck by Nyro's unpretentious persona and unique approach to theme. In an interview with the author on 13 May 2022, Vega elaborates:

Laura Nyro was like a sister figure to me. I was really obsessed with her. Everything from the first song to *Eli and the Thirteenth Confession* and *New York Tendaberry*. I wouldn't say she influenced me because of all she played on the piano, but I loved the way she thought and I love the way that came out in the songs. I loved her inconsistencies and the characters she wrote about. She always wrote about boys named Joe or Tom. I know boys like that. I went to school with them. They were kids I knew too. So, I really loved her for that and I just loved her for who she was. She had the long hair. She was very feminine, very female, whereas I didn't feel very female. I was a more boyish girl. I thought of her as a womanly figure that I would never be. But she wrote about New York and she wrote about sexuality and being a teenage girl and all of the dangers that implied, as well as the thrills, and for that, I was grateful.

Although New York City has traditionally been a tough nut to crack, career-wise, a couple of future allies were scouting out talent.

Enter Steve Addabbo and Ron Fierstein. The college compadres and co-band members had conjured up a master plan; Fierstein was a law school graduate, with an eye for management whilst Addabbo, a recording engineer, doubled as an instrumentalist.

They formally founded AGF Entertainment with the hopes of developing a unique local act. They wouldn't be looking for long – Vega, with her striking looks, unarguable confidence, and army of originals, had the potential to be their winning ticket. In an interview with the author in 2022, Addabbo describes his first impression of Vega:

> I first saw her in Gerdes Folk City in 1983 or so when she was an opening act. She was wearing a tuxedo jacket and singing an *a cappella* tune which we all now know. She was actually playing electric guitar, for some reason, with the bass player, Billy Merchant.

(Merchant lives in New York City and doubles as a luthier. He designed an electric upright bass in the early 1980s. After developing a career repairing double basses in 1977, he acquired a client list which included instrumentalists Charles Mingus and Ron Carter, among others).

Addabbo had 'access to free studio time' because he worked at (the now defunct) Celestial Sounds but needed to tap into the right talent. Vega, the first artist that he and Fierstein came across, had the qualities that the team was seeking. She was well worth the gamble. Addabbo:

> She had really good stage presence immediately, even though she was pretty young. In 1983, she was about 23 or 24. She had this interesting voice; the songs seemed interesting, too. It wasn't like we were looking for somebody that had a hit record with me. We were more into developing an artist, getting somebody a record deal.

The three professionals had their work cut out for them; each musician was learning and growing. Would their two-way street union be riddled with gridlock? Time would tell.

Fierstein and Addabbo held that their chosen artist had the right professional attributes, but they still had to earn her trust and prove their worth. Addabbo recalled:

> There was a definite path. You made demos, shopped it around. You got rejected; you try again. At first, she looked at us, like, 'What have you guys done?' We'd been in our own band. I'd been engineering, but as a producer, I hadn't really made my mark yet.

Addabbo had largely been working with indie bands, but he was enthusiastic and open to ideas concerning working with a solo artist. He instinctively told Vega: 'Come down to the studio. No strings attached. Sit down and play some songs. We'll see what happens.'

Vega committed to visiting Addabbo at Celestial Sounds weeks later. What might have been construed as a casual invite, she took seriously. Addabbo:

She sat down and played about eight or nine songs for the first record; just one after another. She was really professional; her guitar style and her voice were unique. We hit it off. She liked what I did in the studio. I don't think she'd ever heard herself over the big studio monitors. It went really well and from there on we started working together, playing on demos.

Addabbo began gigging with Vega, and along with good friend and guitarist Jonathan Gordon, they formed a solid trio which became 'the first incarnation of the Suzanne Vega Band.'

The trio played mostly at Gerdes Folk City and The Bottom Line. Addabbo: 'That's when we started getting a little buzz going because it was a very fresh sound.' Although Addabbo was aware of the degree to which labels chose to categorize artists, and that Vega frequented folk clubs, he remained cognizant of his new client's unique abilities and refused to pigeon-hole her. He seemingly foresaw a future in which the ambitious Vega could take off in any number of musical directions. Addabbo confirmed:

I never considered Suzanne to be a folk singer. She was writing a much more modern style of music at the time. We clicked. She liked what I did to her music. Making an album made everything more complete.

Meanwhile, Addabbo delved deeply into his client's arrangements. Vega's unique guitar-playing style 'left a lot of room to put stuff around.' The obvious choices were guitar and bass, but synthesizers were becoming increasingly en vogue on the American airwaves by virtue of The Simple Minds, Prince and Madonna. As mentioned previously, the neo-folk era was described by many critics as a second wave of folk music, but it also followed that these acoustic artists had more access to technology than their counterparts.

Plus, Greenwich Village had a theoretical built-in audience; students and teachers from New York University and The New School, and a constant stream of tourists could be at their beck and call if they were dealt the right hand. Vega created physical mailing lists – there was no such thing as 'social media' back then – but expectations were high that a fusion of the old and new would attract an audience.

Still, Vega had been largely accustomed to a subtle sound. That being said, she had to adjust when the team insisted on bringing in unwieldy drum machines. This must have seemed like a stretch for a self-taught musician, who had been creating her own dynamics by virtue of a forceful strum, muted strings, or the precise pressure of a thumb pic. She'd played with powerful bassists, but that accompaniment could be characterized as an organic sound. Moreover, some of the other club entertainers regarded the drum machine and synthesizer with disdain, 'even though,' according to Addabbo, 'we only used it on one or two songs.'

Despite objections, Vega went full speed ahead with the program, putting faith in her colleagues. Addabbo recalled: 'She was supportive of me and the whole label developing stuff.'

They produced demos in Addabbo's living room four-track when they couldn't gain access to Celestial Sound. When time permitted, they sought out sidemen.

As far as accumulating audience leads, promotion meant literally pounding the pavement. Addabbo describes the tedious 'shopping in the traditional sense,' which was the *modus operandi* of that era: 'In those days, you'd take demos around, knock on doors, try to make A & R (artist and repertoire) contacts. I had a few at first. So, that was the beginning of the actual studio work.'

In a *Classic Pop* article from 12 July 2017, 'Vive La Vega – Suzanne Vega Interview', Vega lamented the arduous waiting game the team endured: 'We worked on those tapes and sent them, not only to A&M but to all the big labels. All of them said 'no', including A&M. They said 'no' twice.'

It ultimately took a positive review from *New York Times* music critic Stephen Holden to get both A&M and David Geffen's label riled up enough to approach Vega and her team in 1984, which then created, according to Vega in the same article: 'a nice little bidding war.'

L. A. arranger/composer John Philip Shenale remembers A&M providing a congenial working environment for its artists:

> I spent a lot of time at A&M Studios in the 80s and 90s while it was still owned by Alpert and Moss. I remember working in Studio C, a small pre-production and overdub room, and during a playback of what I had just recorded, I felt someone in the back of me. It was Herb Alpert moving with the track, playing and smiling, and then, he just snuck out the back. Herb liked checking in and hearing what was going on at A&M. He promoted a pro-artist and pro-production feeling in the complex. It became a sort of Audio Engineering University. So many great records were made there. So many engineers learned their craft there.

As a poetic lyricist, melody maker and evocative guitarist, Vega was a self-contained act and it was imperative for a production team to respect her creative boundaries. She would hand-pick producers down the road, but early studio albums were crucial calling cards. Addabbo envisioned the partnership through a production prism that wouldn't cramp her style:

'Suzanne didn't need us. She could do it by herself and it was very complete sounding. So, the record, it needed some edge, it needed some drums, it needed some electric guitars…'

The solid work that the team pored into the demos would sometimes result in a completed track; Addabbo recalled that their final version of 'Cracking' 'is actually the demo.' (Addabbo elaborates further under that entry).

Early guitarist Jonathan Gordon was highly influential in Vega's career. In an interview with the author on 10 June 2022, Gordon discussed his own background and how he tailored his playing to Vega's musical stories. Prior to their partnership, he played sessions with Madonna and country bands and toured with former Peter, Paul and Mary lead vocalist Mary Travers. Gordon recalled:

In terms of my work with Suzanne, I tried to play in a lot of different styles, but I needed to develop a little vocabulary; translating my work to the context of Suzanne. When I first saw her, she worked with a band and performed with nothing, really, any bigger than a two-guitar duo. I felt that what I brought to the table… I had to play much more minimalist, quieter, more sensitive stuff than I had in other contexts. In terms of specific references that I had, I think the three players that stood out in terms of my defining approach to Suzanne had been Andy Summers of The Police, The Edge and Mark Knopfler. Those are the ones who spring to mind in terms of what I was using as a reference. 'Luka' definitely had an 'Edge' kind of sensibility to it. I got involved with Suzanne when Steve Addabbo and Ron Fierstein were forming a company to manage and produce her. I actually knew Steve from country western bands, among other things. He thought I might be a good fit to work with Suzanne. The first time I saw her perform would have been at Gerde's Folk City on West 3rd or 4th.

Seeing Vega live helped Gordon formulate an action plan for arrangement purposes:

It was an intimate room, you could get maybe 100 people in. You could hear a pin drop and Suzanne came out as a solo. She completely mesmerized and killed the plaything and I was really, really impressed with her. Certainly, in that kind of atmosphere, in that intimate crowd, in a very quiet venue, she could just hold peoples' attention. I felt that was really essential to what she was. So, my job, as I saw it, with working with her, was to scale what I was doing to what she was doing; to complement her, not get overly loud; fill out a lot of the sounds without disturbing what I saw as the essential core of it.

Gordon elaborated on the studio sessions strategies:

Suzanne and I would sort of be the core of the song. Other people would add other stuff around that. In a couple of cases, I had a lot of influence on what other people were adding to the song. In other words, I was involved in some of the arranging of the songs. And in others, it was less.

As producer, how would Richard Barone approach Vega?

I would work on an arrangement that would work on every aspect of her voice. She has a beautiful texture in the tone of her voice. I would just focus everything around that. And I'm not trying to say that Lenny (Kaye) or Steve (Addabbo) or any of her other producers have not done that but I would just start fresh and approach it directly from the sound of her voice.

We discussed Richard Barone's memories of the Village when Vega got started. Barone's album, *Sorrows and Promises: Greenwich Village in the 1960s* (2016), featured reimagined covers. Barone replied to the question: Which song from that album would Suzanne Vega do best?

I think she would do a beautiful version – she might have even done this at some point – of 'Sunday Morning' by the Velvet Underground. I think her voice would just envelop that melody, and that song crosses over a few different things. Even though it's a Velvet Underground song, it has a lot of traditional folk elements in it and a little Simon and Garfunkel in it. I think she would really deliver a great performance. That's the first thing that comes to mind because of what we've talked about but she could do any of those songs because we have that thread of knowing the past of Greenwich Village.

Similarly, to Vega, Barone often designates New York City's brick and mortar as a muse:

I'm looking out of my window at Waverly Place. The buildings are from the 1800s, and there's a timelessness that comes through the architecture of The Village. If you're around it all the time, or often, it certainly affects how you think about things. You're not just writing for the moment, you're writing for a longer period of time, knowing that something can be timeless.

There's a strong wave of synchronicity that permeates Vega's world. Broadcaster Pete Fornatale's resonant voice popularized *Mixed Bags* concerts in Greenwich Village, a project which he conceptualized in 1982, and for decades afterward on stations WFUV, WNEW and WXRX. After being inspired by a fan letter Vega sent, Fornatale eagerly promoted her music, and that of contemporaries Shawn Colvin and John Gorka, among others, for years to come.

While Vega's admiration of her predecessors undoubtedly informed her approach to writing, she has also kept an open mind to non-western philosophy. As such, Vega and her family practiced a form of Buddhism based on the teachings of the 13th-century Buddhist priest, Nichiren, which includes the chanting of the mantra, 'Nam Myoho Renge Kyo' and reading from Sanskrit scriptures as a means of attaining spiritual enlightenment and creating an overall sense of well-being. To *Under the Radar*, Vega described this form of Buddhism as:

...a very concrete practice, which I find particularly helpful. You do the prayers twice a day, they're said out loud, and you chant to an object of worship, a scroll (a Gohonzon) that you receive. You chant to yourself and you chant for others because it's not always about you, so I found this to be a great venue for hopes and dreams and wishes and prayers and all these things.

This revitalized philosophy has attracted myriad artists; some continue the practice, while others satisfied their curiosity for a concentrated period of time. Tina Turner, Herbie Hancock, Laurie Anderson, REM's Michael Stipe and the late songwriter Leonard Cohen are entertainers who either practiced or are still practicing Nichiren Buddhism.

You'll (hopefully) discover after reading *On Track: Suzanne Vega* that her repertoire has been earmarked by substantial growth, be it spiritual, developmental, cognitive or purely artistic.

Author's Note

We'll explore Vega's complete discography: studio albums, acoustic albums, compilations, live albums and extended plays. Singles relative to each album will be included in their respective sections. I won't dwell on live concerts or videos but will cite them if relevant.

I have spent exponentially more time on specific tracks and/or introductions than on others, if certain material warrants deeper analysis. In part, my choices will be contingent upon stories, anecdotes and opinions from other professionals: musicians, producers, label owners, etc., who have generously provided first-hand source material for this book, but I also drew upon interviews that I conducted in coordination with *pennyblackmusic.co.uk*. over a series of years as a staff journalist.

Suzanne Vega (1985)

Personnel:
Suzanne Vega: vocals (1-10), acoustic guitar (1-10)
Steve Addabbo: background vocals (4, 5, 7), synclavier guitar (6), twelve-string acoustic guitar (8), electric guitar (10)
Darol Anger: electric violin (7)
Frank Christian: acoustic guitar (2, 9), electric slide guitar (10)
Paul Dugan: bass (1, 4, 6, 8, 9), vertical bass (2),
Sue Evans: drums (3, 5, 6, 10), percussion (4, 10)
Jon Gordon: electric guitar (1-7)
Peter Gordon: string arrangement (6)
Frank Gravis: bass (3, 5, 10)
Shem Guibbory: violin (6)
Mark Isham: synthesizers (7)
John Mahoney: synclavier programming (6)
Maxine Neuman: cello (6)
C.P. Roth: synthesizers (1-5, 9), piano (8), organ (8)
Roger Squitero: percussion (7)
Label: A&M
Produced at Celestial Sound, New York City by Steve Addabbo and Lenny Kaye on 1 May 1985
Release date: 1 May 1985
Highest chart places: UK (OCC): 11, US Billboard 200: 91, NZL: 9, AUS: 23
Running time: 35:37
Album Art: In Charles Reilly's image, Vega stands in front of a window with chalk-white blinds. Waif-like, with strands of ginger hair overlapping one eye, she's, curiously, captured in the shadows. Her facial expression registers little emotion, but ironically, this tabula rasa effect allows our imaginations to soar. This modest artist, in a buttoned-down shirt and black jacket with broad lapels, has something to say, yet remains at arms-length. We've not been spoon-fed what Suzanne Vega's about. We are being trusted to come to our own conclusions.

Vega told *Washington Post* writer Richard Harrington on 6 November 1985: 'It's hard for me to work on the lyrics separately from the music.' Vega's capability to tackle melody and lyrics simultaneously is, for her fans, a blessing, because that cohesiveness comes across very effectively on this debut recording.

Despite being armed with a serious arsenal of originals, the prospect of recording an album was daunting: 'I was nervous making it and I was nervous after it was out,' she admitted.

As a mid-1980s female guitarist and singer-songwriter, comparisons by the popular press to Vega's peers and predecessors were imminent. Where would she fit within the spectrum? Based on her poetic bent, would she be branded as the new Patti Smith? Would her deeply personal, and often sanguine reflections trigger thoughts of classic Joni Mitchell? Tori Amos?

Vega had reason to buckle under pressure from the press. Reviewers often felt obligated to draw comparisons when a new female artist entered the public arena. In fact, even if the other acts weren't mentioned, the media elephant monopolized the room. If the reader also liked the critic's referenced act, the female artist might fare well. If not, well …

As such, *allmusic.com* juxtaposed Vega's interpretive style with that of 1960s folk singer Janis Ian, an alumnus of Vega's high school, and of 'Society's Child' and 'At Seventeen' fame: 'Like Ian, she sings with a precise, frequently spoken half-spoken phrasing that gives her lyrics an intensity that seems to suggest an unsteady control consciously held over emotional chaos'. In that same article, *allmusic.com* compared Vega's poetic output to that of muse Leonard Cohen.

There *were* similarities: both singers generally kept a handle on their emotions and allowed the lyrics to do the heavy lifting. You'd hear few histrionics (from either chanteuse) that color or distract from the experience, and there was generally a linear follow-through in both of their approaches: the story invariably came first.

A new act had to contend with traditional studio pressures, such as being subject to a high degree of quality control, budget monitoring and tight deadlines.

Co-producer Lenny Kaye had had considerable experience both in and out of the studio prior to taking on Vega's project. He'd gained knowledge of popular culture throughout the 1970s by being a reviewer for *Rolling Stone*, *Crawdaddy* and *Fusion*, a freelancer for *Melody Maker* and *Creem* and editor for *Hit Parader.*

Kaye produced Patti Smith's *Hey Joe/Piss Factory* and was her guitarist in the Patti Smith Group for four albums produced between 1975 and 1979: *Horses*, *Radio Ethiopia*, *Easter* and *Wave*. In 1995, when he and Smith reunited, he resumed his role as guitarist in her band.

For 'How Lenny Kaye, The Godfather of Garage Rock Illuminated 'The Psalms'' by Bob Boilen on *npr.org* from 24 March 2017, Kaye articulated his basic production philosophy:

> You're not trying to steer something in a direction. You're not trying to analyze the song. You choose musicians who you feel are empathetic with what you're doing and allow them to express themselves. Perhaps you move things here or there, or you suggest an idea or two, but the process is very organic and that's the way I like it.

He developed strengths that clients already had and mainstreamed technical and instrumental effects: 'I think that as a producer, you frame the artist with sounds that embrace her in a certain way. You just want to find textures that let the song express itself.'

Commenting on Vega's performance of 'Luka', Kaye said: 'In a way, Suzanne's vocal floats over the song... I think Suzanne's almost dispassionate delivery heightens the intent of the song.'

In that broadcast, Kaye mentioned a mid-1990s project with Jessi Colter: 'I'm a Capricorn so I climb the mountain slowly.' Perhaps Kaye eased up during this time, but how slowly could Kaye have climbed, under the stopwatch of a highly competitive record label earlier in his career?

Kaye mentioned feeling wary of professionals who over-analyzed their clients' output lest they 'take the charm and the magic out of it.' And history proved, that when he'd worked as a thrashing guitarist with a brawling Patti Smith on *Horses,* he co-created a punk rock hallmark.

Needless to say, Kaye instinctively recognized a good hook and an infectious beat; but putting commercial creativity aside, producing a debut also requires paying strict attention to logistical tasks, as well as establishing mutually acceptable boundaries between artist and client.

Co-producer Steve Addabbo *was* understandably concerned about staying within the recording budget and ensuring the efficiency of the final product. But at times, there was a battle of creative wills. In an interview with the author, Addabbo said: 'There were two or three songs on the first album, and I felt she didn't do the best she could; Suzanne thought it was fine, but I thought, 'No, you can do better.''

Despite a few contentious moments, both Vega and Addabbo were motivated to achieve a similar goal. It was merely a matter of how to get there: 'I'd make her go back and sing, and she'd get rather frustrated and say, 'No, I'm not really mad, but I've had enough.'' he recounted, 'At one point, she walked downstairs to the lounge, but left her shoes in the control room so had to come back in.'

Fortunately, neither party caved under the pressure and both remained open to innovation. Addabbo:

I said, 'Suzanne, try this.' I had the track and was asking her to sing the vocal again. It wasn't quite right. I finally said, 'Sit and put your guitar on until you feel more comfortable; just put your guitar on and you don't have to play it.' She thought that was the dumbest idea ever; she said, 'Why do I have to do this?'

Vega's guitar, being more than a material means of expression, doubled as an ad hoc prop, which was not necessarily a negative thing: imagine Groucho Marx sans cigar, Liberace without a glittery jacket, or Linus, from the American comic strip, *Peanuts*, without his blanket – but in the studio, the guitar was a nemesis. Vega was accustomed to playing live with her guitar, a constant companion, but the instrument often hindered her ability to perform studio tasks.

In fact, Vega would later say that learning to move on the stage in front of the mic without her guitar presented an actual challenge, one which often mystified journalists because she had expressed herself freely onstage as a dancer, but performing as a musician was different. She had to concentrate fully to play the guitar, and so moving away from the instrument and then locking fingers back into position to form shapes often interrupted her focus.

A further challenge was that the recording studio may have felt like an alien place; a warehouse of tangled wires and insulated walls, containing none of the warmth she'd felt radiating from a rapt audience in an animated coffee house setting.

Vega would have cultivated that comfort at the completely student-run Postcrypt Coffeehouse, where Friday and Saturday night concerts featured 45-50-minute sets by a trio of fresh voices. Although the atmosphere was welcoming, the club was by no means fancy. *The New York Times* referred to the weekend comfort zone as 'a musty hideaway.'

The cramped space needed no microphones and, in fact, had little room for more than the most basic setup. Located in the basement of St. Paul's Chapel, founded in 1964 and owned by Columbia University, occupancy was restricted to 35 people.

Student management sometimes-locked horns with Columbia University powers-that-be when they utilized cheap, potentially hazardous candles in lieu of more expensive lighting, but in their defense, students were simply trying to make ends meet.

Jeff Buckley, David Bromberg and Ani DiFranco were among Postcrypt's other acclaimed benefactors. Remarkably, the club is still going strong today, and every so often, Vega pops in to make a surprise appearance.

Back to the restrictive studio setting: the clock behind the glass wall ticked with a vengeance, and at times, Addabbo was desperate to move things along: 'Just do it,' he pleaded. 'Dumb idea,' notwithstanding, Vega was a team player. She strapped on the guitar, leaving Addabbo to carefully tape up the strings 'so that they wouldn't sound.' With the immediate issue solved, the co-producer was elated: 'She's holding it, and within 40 minutes, I had all three songs.'

Addabbo confirmed:

It just relaxed her. It was like body posture. It's a little awkward, especially when you're young, singing with headphones on. There was no support system. So, I figured if she was wearing her guitar, she'd have something to hold on to and it worked. It was definitely on 'Knight Moves,' and I don't remember the other two. It makes a difference on a record like that to have a vocal that is spotless, not exactly perfect, but that has the right delivery. I just felt we didn't have it on the other takes.

As co-producer, Addabbo was as privy to mounting pressures as any other first-time producer in the competitive popular music industry: 'Lenny was supportive, too. Suzanne was getting mad at us, and Lenny would start to lose it, and then we got it. I've often said, 'desperation is the mother of invention.''

Although Vega may have held both producers in high esteem, she likely sensed that, as a new team, they would be testing the waters as they learned to accommodate each other, but there were bound to be conflicts. She told Cindy Stagoff in 'Suzanne Vega will livestream New York Songs from Powerful New Album to the World' at *njarts.com* on 2 October 2020:

> ...we definitely had our moments when we were making our first album and then our second album: a lot of creative tensions. And I didn't have the vocabulary to really lead them. All I could do is say, 'I like it' or 'I don't like it' or 'Why is this so loud?'

When Addabbo exclaimed: 'Desperation is the mother of invention,' did he anticipate that the desperation would pay off so handsomely? Whatever uncertainties the team underwent during the pre-production, production and post-production process, they achieved considerable acclaim.

Suzanne Vega is listed at number 80 on the *Rolling Stone* 1989 list of '100 Best Albums of the Eighties,' cited in *1001 Albums You Must Hear Before You Die* and achieved platinum status in the UK for the sale of 300,000 units and 250,000 in the US.

'Cracking' (Suzanne Vega)

This opener's apocalyptic theme belies Vega's cavalier vocals. While the words describe, as the title suggests, an emotional meltdown, the casual intonation borders on whimsy. We can easily connect the dots between the 1970s Lou Reed concert she attended and the effect his work had on her storytelling approach thereafter.

Vega told *The Times* on 2 November 2013: 'Lou Reed changed my life – artistically and actually.' Watching the former Velvet Underground frontman perform in 1979 was liberating for the then-Barnard college student; that exposure led Vega to shake off the stereotypical folk image with which she'd been initially branded. In an interview with Reed, he implied that the industry had unfairly typecast Vega as a folk singer. She would eventually cover Reed's 'Walk on the Wild Side' and sound every bit as natural as her muse.

The easy-going patter that Vega evokes here awakened my empathy for the 'Cracking' subject, a protagonist who is obviously overwhelmed, and relatedly human. This is a deeply personal song, flush with sensitive 'I' statements, but at the chorus, Vega retreats to melismatic 'ah's' sung in her upper register, with phrases beginning on a suspended chord. Because her head voice is, arguably, thinner than her contralto, this section reveals an even greater degree of vulnerability. And because the lyrics of the verse are so linear and palpable: 'my footsteps are ticking/the sun is blinding,' the 'ah's' offer a cleansing breath from the lockstep.

But the chorus stands on its own melodically and harmonically, and like so much of Vega's work, this song follows the 'less is more' philosophy of songwriting, with subtle statements that require little elaboration, and slight, but poignant variations in the harmonic structure.

Addabbo recalled:

When we first started this process, I had Jon Gordon playing electric guitar; I didn't play on that track. We had done that, and a couple of other songs that were part of the demo, and then when we got the record deal, we said, 'now we're going to do the real version; the full version.' So, we did another version of 'Cracking', and somehow, it just wasn't as good. It just didn't have the edge, and so, even though the first demo was not as technically perfect, maybe, it just had a vibe to it, so that was the one we actually used on the record.

'Freeze Tag' (Suzanne Vega)

The title, inspired by a popular, interactive American schoolyard game, involves a child being designated as 'it'. This child's task is to tag other children, who then must stand still until being 'unfrozen' by other 'unfrozen' players.

'Freeze Tag' is an invigorating, uncomplicated game that allows children to burn off energy and reach a common goal, but in this case, it is also a celebration of Vega's courtship to attorney and poet, Paul Mills, her husband of many years.

On 'Adele: The '30 Interview" in November 2021, the Australian vocalist/ songwriter relayed to Zane Lowe that her mother comforted her with Vega's song: "Freeze Tag' used to be the lullaby that she'd sing to me if I couldn't sleep.'

The minor-to-major chords and Frank Christian's piercing melodic line in the introduction foreshadow the song's bittersweet nature. Despite the playground equipment terms and Adele's primal recollections, I can't qualify 'Freeze Tag' as a lullaby; it's much too mature in theme, although it does have a tender, sing-song quality that a child can easily remember. I believe the song moves along much too briskly to qualify in that category, although the pretty voicings and Vega's warm performance might theoretically soothe a crabby child.

Vega's voice slides comfortably against the roiling chords and remains fluid over a sudden but refreshing tempo change. Shawn Colvin contributes to the pleasing background. That contagious minor-major dichotomy continues throughout.

In the first verses, Vega creates an immediate air of mystery by using two characters to move the story forward. Vega cleverly masks their motivations and true identities, leaving us to ponder: Are they adults reviving their childhood? Or are they children being safeguarded by an omniscient protector like Holden Caulfield, the protagonist in *Catcher in the Rye*, who wants to help all children retain their innocence before entering the often-harsh adult world?

Vega personifies and assigns adult agency to the standard playground equipment, as the two explore their surroundings, through 'slides into the past' and 'swings of indecision.' The term 'Freeze tag' acquires a deeper meaning, too, through the initial consonant alliteration of 'tingling and trembling.' The innocent game becomes caustic, eliciting a gnawing sense of fear.

In the second verse, as the two-play act, they assign each other actual roles, much as engaged children in the playground often do, but these roles involve sensual, romantic Hollywood leads: 'I will be Dietrich, you will be Dean.' Vega references glamorous German-born actress Marlene Dietrich and *Rebel Without a Cause* heartthrob James Dean, who died in a car crash.

Vega's crooning reference: 'You will be Bogart and I will be Bacall' circles back in time to actor Humphrey Bogart, famous for playing toughs, and the sophisticated Lauren Bacall, who were once romantically, and somewhat scandalously, linked (we get less access to Dietrich in 'Freeze Tag,' but get to obsess on the following song, 'Marlene on the Wall'). There is considerably more lyrical movement in the two rapidly sung bridges.

Finally, the guitar work in the outro is stunning – it's an immutable wrap. Addabbo was elated:

> The feeling was so well-captured. I don't know how we did it, but we did it. 'Freeze Tag' and 'Small Blue Thing'; those songs just added a level of space around them. They had very evocative lyrics and were very visual. They were descriptive, which is what Suzanne does best.
> Both songs came across. We didn't get in her way. They're really interesting. It's not just a girl and her guitar. There's a little atmosphere around those songs that enhances it and doesn't get in her way; it doesn't draw attention to herself, but it's like, 'wow.'

Gordon approached this track similar to the way that he approached 'Small Blue Thing.' His unobtrusive, electronic detail is atmospheric and dreamily mysterious. Moreover, Vega and Gordon show an impressive amount of restraint in their execution.

'Marlene on the Wall' (Suzanne Vega)
Single release: UK: 83, re-release: UK: 21, IRE: 9, AUS: 39

Addabbo:

> This was the last song that Suzanne wrote for the album. It's got a strange beat. We didn't know what it was. It wasn't like a straight backbeat. I

remember Suzanne playing acoustic on that, and thinking this is really very cool. It was the most poppy song. I guess, it was the first single from that record. It didn't do really well here, but it did very well in England. It made it to about 21. It was a pretty big hit in Europe. It was a true story. Suzanne had someone over and 'Marlene' was looking at her from the poster. That song connected with the past but it was really fresh. It was kind of a fun one to do. The drum parts were not traditional. The bass part was not traditional. The guy Lenny brought in just couldn't cut it, so I brought in a bass player. When Frank Gravis came to the studio, it really helped that song gel. Rhythmically, that was a strange song to produce, but I really like the way it came out.

Gordon:

Suzanne was frustrated and on the verge of dropping the song. I said, 'You can't drop it because it's an up-tempo song in a major key and you have hardly any of those.' Strategically, it was an important song for her because it was a hit in Europe before a lot of stuff happened with her in the States. The other thing was, I just felt that that song was a declaration of independence on her part about changing her destiny. I felt that song came when Suzanne was finding her power and her agency. There were certainly things in that song that spoke to me about starting to feel empowered, you know, so I like that about the song a lot. It was an exciting song to play. But the way that I think I saved it, was that nobody knew what kind of drum beat to put to it. When we were first starting to rehearse it in the studio – Sue Evans was a wonderful drummer, but she was hearing it as a two-beat, boom chick, boom chick. The result of it would have been kind of corny so I went home and mulled the whole thing over and came up with an idea. Listen to the chorus. It has an odd drumbeat. Basically, that was my work. I was taking stylistic direction from reggae stuff, in reaction to a lot of what Stewart Copeland was doing in The Police. I think his inspiration was also reggae stuff, a lot of trademark stuff, like putting the bass drum where the snare would have been, not playing on the downbeat. That weird drumbeat was basically what I came up with and brought to rehearsal and said, 'Sue, try this.' We reorganized some stuff around it. From the standpoint of what the rhythm section was doing, it ended up as a half-time with an implied double-time feel, and one of the things that helped to imply the double-time was that there's an accent that happens right after the missing downbeat: tick a bom. That tick thing, which keeps the double-time sense going on, became an accent that both me and the synthesizer play. So, I sat there in rehearsal and said, 'Let's try it this way.' That's what we ended up recording. The reason the song ended up with the kind of rhythmic feel that it did was because I workshopped and then brought something into rehearsal.

'Marlene on The Wall' stands out instrumentally due to the quirky rhythm that Gordon detailed, but the storyline also intrigues. When Vega sings: 'She recalls the rise and fall of every soldier passing,' she's referencing the late Dietrich's support of the US during World War II. Vega made the story pop, too, by fusing the legacy of the influential female icon with a contemporary, coming-of-age theme.

In an author interview in 2012, Vega reiterated: 'Yes, the point of view is Marlene's image – watching the girl I once was in my room. But I still feel it when I sing the lines, 'I think it's called my destiny that I'm changing.' I still feel that.'

'Small Blue Thing' (Suzanne Vega)
Single release: UK: 65

In an author interview in 2012, I asked Vega if there was a spiritual side to 'Small Blue Thing':

> I was more trying to convey a sense of sensuality, I suppose, which could be intertwined with spirituality. For some people and for me that's definitely true. So, there's kind of a borderline, I guess. For me, that wasn't specifically what I was going for, but I would say it's expressed in it.

To me, 'Small Blue Thing' is sonic origami; a haunting think piece which the discriminating listener can unfold and re-examine in a variety of ways: one Chicago aficionado implied that it is an ode to Mother Earth and its pedestrian role in a vast, seemingly endless universe.

Another saw the narrator as a vulnerable child, seeking security: 'I am lost inside your pocket.' Others ascertain that the theme serves as a sounding board for domestic abuse survivors: 'I am falling down the stairs...'

In interviews, Vega has stated a number of motivations for writing 'Small Blue Thing,' which include: viewing objects in space as 'geometric', constructing an authentic love song, and expressing her views on gender identity.

On 12 October 2016, Vega told *Rolling Stone* that, for a certain period in her life, 'I did not like being female, being a girl... I wanted to be something other than that, not necessarily male – if I could have been a thing or a plant or anything...'

Fittingly, Vega related strongly to author Carson McCullers's work, as well, due to the southern author's 'gender fluidity'. Later, we'll look at Vega's own spin on McCullers's writings.

While over the years, Vega has admitted to masking the meaning of her music, with the hopes that fans will bring their own experiences to her songs, 'Small Blue Thing' could arguably be the template, as it lends itself to multiple, complex interpretations.

In regards to real-time, the first sentence suggests, to me, the principle of Zen impermanence: 'Today I am a small blue thing.' I once saw a Buddhist monk painstakingly construct a beautiful sand mandala. Afterwards, he blew away the particles and said that he felt no regret because that act of closure represented freedom from material entanglement. In 'Small Blue Thing', time is blurred and suspended, with no mention of tomorrow or the near future.

But there is a shift in mood. In the second verse, and in Vega's continued song whisperer mode, the lyric momentarily borders on fear, when she purrs: 'I am watching you', yet quickly, the entities unite, and we're enmeshed in a fragile love song: 'I am cold against your skin. You are perfectly reflected.' While there is no actual mention of gender or romantic love, arrows certainly point to a tender, respectful and consensual relationship.

Vega's precise word choices bear mention, too. The repetitive phrase: 'Scattering like light', is attractive to the ear, not only because of the obvious alliteration but because the gerund 'scattering' hits the mark so well. While the word 'shattering' would also fit the melody, that modifier has an aggressive tone – 'scattering' elicits a delicate effect. Lithe on the ear, easy on the teeth, the word embodies what Chicago songwriter Ralph Covert calls, 'mouth feel'.

In the final verse, Vega reveals: 'I never blink'. Could this be an example of hyper-vigilance on the part of a vulnerable victim? Or an assertion of discipline and authority? 'Small Blue Thing' oozes with linear mystery.

Regarding the instrumental arrangement of 'Small Blue Thing', Addabbo said:

I had that idea for that lick in there. Charlie Roth, one of Lenny Kaye's guys, was a really great keyboard player. It was very delicate to add that stuff to what Suzanne was doing, and not make it sound hokey or retro or forced. It was not just, 'oh, let's do this', it took a lot of finessing to find the right sound and mix it just right so it didn't interfere with her. What's great about Suzanne's guitar playing is that it's not really strummy... Now, 'Marlene on the Wall' was, but on most of the other stuff, she left a lot of space and room to add some color. Instead of filling out all of the spaces, you're finding it and doing it. When you're there, there's no real grand plan: 'No, that doesn't sound good. That sounds corny.' I was really trying to find stuff that wasn't cliché to put in there.

Vega remembered: 'I'm trying to express an image or idea. It's not just a feeling. There's something behind it that I'm trying to express.' In contrast, Vega approaches 'character songs' through a different lens:

I would try to find out what language that character would use, how old is that character, is it male or female? Whereas a song like 'Small Blue Thing' is more abstract. If I were an animation or a cartoon, how would I feel?

In an interview with the author on 15 January 2014, Vega elaborated:

> The item that inspired that song was a ceramic doorknob that had a blue eye on it in my old boyfriend's apartment. I can't explain how the creative process works, but somehow that ended up being the inspiration. But it was mostly the feeling of being in his hand that inspired that song. It's a love song to that man.

Over the course of Vega's career, fans have scrutinized her lyrics. Responses to abstract tunes, like 'Small Blue Thing', can result in the songwriter throwing up her hands:

> People are constantly saying, 'Is that a riddle?' or 'What do you really mean?' People will ask me weird questions like, 'Is that a fetus?' No, it is not a fetus for obvious reasons. But people think what they think, and some people really get metaphor and other people just don't.

'Straight Lines' (Suzanne Vega)
Addabbo:

> We'd been playing live as a trio: me, Suzanne and Jon Gordon, and so a lot of those parts developed. It wasn't like we came up with them in the studio. It wasn't like, 'we've got to put something in here.'

Gordon said that 'Straight Lines' felt like two separate songs. The lyrical gentleness: 'The golden light of the morning', contrasted with a fiery background. Did he intentionally follow Vega's vocal lines closely with his guitar?

> I was working very hard to come up with something definitive, I was just concentrating on trying to execute it perfectly every time. There were some elements of improvisation coming up, but once I come up with the parts: okay, this is it. This is the best I can do with this. I just maintain it and I have to do it consistently. By the time we were on stage, I wasn't improvising. I was trying to recreate whatever I had done, as faithfully as I could.

'Straight Lines' strikes an illuminating balance between Vega's persuasive voice and the palpable instrumental track. In the chorus, the clarity of her instrument against the pounding rhythm section is sublime. The line, 'cold metal close to the bone' ushers in Sue Evans' angry drums and Frank Gravis' distinctive bass. Charlie Roth's synth colors the first five tracks of the album; his work here adds a crucial ethereal edge. Addabbo's backing vocals add a contrasting brush stroke. Finally, the arrangement allows adequate space for lead vocals in the outro.

'Undertow' (Suzanne Vega)
Addabbo:

'Undertow' was a tricky son-of-a-gun, one of my favorites at the time – it still is. Sometimes, we thought we'd put a little too much stuff in there, maybe there is. The chord changes, perhaps? It was really one of my favorites, but then, when it came time to do it, it was a very hard track to pull off. I think the strings were A&M's ideas. At one point, I thought, 'we're stuffing too much stuff into this, it's really a hard one to mix', but I also remember that it was experimental.

I played a synth clavier guitar part with this descending line, which was beautiful. I still like it, but I remember that being one of the more complex puzzles of the record. On one hand, it could have been one of the more perceptive rock arrangements, but somehow, I don't remember all the dynamics of how that came about, but it was such a powerful song to me. Not that it was going to be a hit single, but the construction of the song itself, to me, was beautiful and I wanted to make it as grand as we could without screwing it up. I think we were just on the borderline of screwing it up!

Gordon:

Somehow it had been thrown out to a lot of different people who came and did things for it. I probably played whatever I played based on what we'd been performing. They brought in guitar, synthesizers, and Steve played stuff; the arrangement got futzed with a lot.

I imagined 'Undertow' flourishing in a score for a backlit film noir because the words cut dark and deep, especially: 'I would leave only bones and teeth', and 'a bullet in flight'. Strains of bubbling synth, edgy guitar and pin-drop bass frame the white-knuckle phrases. Vega's cool voice stands in opposition to the icy imagery. She's the quintessential forensic agent reporting at the crime scene.

'Some Journey' (Suzanne Vega)
Was the record label offer of guest artists an olive branch or a sandbag?
Addabbo:

When you have an A & R department, they feel like they have to do their job, help with suggestions. So, there was Darol Anger, and the whole group from Wyndham Hill, a subsidiary of A&M, which had all of these great musicians, and A&M said, 'Why don't you do these tracks and we'll invite some of these talented people in?' Okay... The song sticks out a little bit to me. It's got amazing musicianship; the song comes through, but with the travails of working with an A & R department, they try to put their stamp on it. Just leave us alone. Steve Miller, I think, was connected with Wyndham Hill. He's a cool guy, a great engineer. He came in and we mixed it with him. But that was a complicated one to weed out because it's very different from the rest of the record.

Gordon:

Suzanne and I did what we basically did and then sent it out to another production team that arranged a bunch of synthesizers around it. I played what I imagined the part to be, the core of the song. Suzanne played. It went elsewhere to have a bunch of stuff added to it.

'I could've played your little girl or I could have played your wife', Vega spins, before ticking off alternative scenarios with 20/20 hindsight. Yet this song doesn't feel weighed down by bittersweet regrets. It appears to be more about a reimagined existence, an honest reflection of a passage of time from an observant narrator.

Harmonically, tension is created through the liberal use of suspended and altered chords in the verses and a hard-boiled strum. Thematically, the narrator hypothesizes: 'If we had met on some eastbound train...' with the ultimate payoff: 'would you have worn your silken robes?'

'Would you have taken me upstairs and turned the lamplight low?' she asks in the next verse. The hypotheticals create a sense of distance and intrigue.

In the third verse, when she sets up a number of situations that could have happened, but didn't, she casts a cynical look at the roles people play in relationships and the inherent cost.

In the final verse, she faces facts. The couple exists in a contemporary framework. They are not masquerading as other people and they cannot, in real-time, fulfill alternative fantasies, for better or worse. In a nutshell, she concludes: 'there are no shadows here.'

In 'Some Journey', Vega exposes a strong feminist voice in a poetic, insightful manner. True to form, she leaves open a gratuitous space, allowing the listener to ponder: Who are we in relation to others? Who do we become within the confines of a relationship? How do we feel about these transformations?

Production-wise, Addabbo noted that the label insisted on adding guests. This practice sometimes worked in favor of the final mix, but sometimes felt intrusive. In any case, outside decisions invariably altered the studio chemistry. In one specific case, though, it's hard to argue about the decision to add violinist Darol Anger, who adds ferocity near the outro.

US Label Hip Pocket Records released composer Steven Miller long enough to have him add overdubs to the arrangement. Accordingly, Miller also received co-producer credits.

'The Queen and the Soldier' (Suzanne Vega)
Addabbo:

That's one of my favorites, too. When I first heard it, I thought of a twelve-string guitar, a deep organ, a synthesizer, a church organ, and a bazooka, or lute – an instrument that came from that time period. I wanted to convert that into a modern version and I have a demo which I did in my living room on a four-track. It's just Suzanne singing with her guitar, a bass synthesizer, a growling, low-note bass line and my twelve-string. To me, that's still my favorite version but when we went to do it, things changed – 'we should add piano'. I never really liked piano in that song, but that's my own thing, and the organ's pretty cool, but I love that song. When we did it, Suzanne would just do verse after verse after verse. I said, 'Suzanne, the listener needs a break to take it all in. That's why you put the instrumental section in the middle, to kind of give it some release. The lyrics are so intense; let me digest it.' I thought that worked brilliantly. It's such a nice release there and then it comes back in to continue the story. I love the twelve-string on there. It goes so nicely with the song.

'The Queen and the Soldier', a penetrating anti-war song with a pleasing pentameter, is about a soldier confronting an unbending monarch. His character comes through clearly in the second line. I empathized with his unwavering resolve, as he stood trembling outside the monarch's door.

He's comparable to the fictional boxer, 'Rocky Balboa,' another highly principled everyman, except that, we get to rejoice after the Philadelphian becomes a legitimate hero after a series of bloody fights; while we won't see this one triumph, we do see him stand his ground and his: 'I am not fighting for you anymore.'

The queen, despite her powerful stature, slowly unravels: 'But her face was a child's and he thought she would cry, but she closed herself up like a fan.' The soldier's visceral reactions and appraisal of the queen's body language support the rest of the sad story.

Vega's linear lyrics lead us carefully through this dialogue, making us fully aware of the space the contrasting characters occupy and the challenges they face. 'The young queen fixed him with an arrogant eye', hints at the outcome, but the overall interchange keeps us at bay.

The story is structurally unique, too, because Vega creates a concurrent dynamic between subjects, using a device author S. Davis calls a 'split-screen' effect, which directors often use in film to depict opposing points of view.

Songwriter Jimmy Webb created this effect, too, in 'By the Time I Get to Phoenix', where the central character guides the listener through his own emotional exodus but cuts away to his perception of his partner's sense of loss in an act of empathy. Webb illustrates two distinctive perspectives, although the male is clearly more in a position of power than the abandoned female.

Similarly, in 'The Queen and the Soldier,' although the former clearly yields more power than the soldier, Vega's flesh-and-blood monarch ultimately shows flashes of humanity.

The guitar work accents the dramatic moments. Through metaphor, rhyme and alliteration, Vega creates an air-tight story that continues to intrigue fans; some of whom, however, wish that the ending had come out more positively.

'I have swallowed a secret, burning thread. It cuts me inside and often I've bled', is one of the most poetic lines in the song. Apparently, it was based on a true story which had little to do with the queen or the soldier, but that detail, drawn from reality, moved the muse.

Vega told *alextimes.com* on 2 September 2021 that her roommate's cat often chewed on the edge of a curtain 'and she did swallow a thread and she had to be put to sleep.'

'Knight Moves' (Suzanne Vega)
Addabbo: 'That was a hard one. It's kind of a weird song; the rhythm of it. How do you put stuff in there? We had to learn those little cuts.'

While the song is not fluid in the instrumental sense, the payoff is in the mood. Vega's voice floats dreamily over ambient sounds while asking, 'Do you love anyone, do you love me?'

The most engaging harmonic elements occur at the bridge, where a series of suspended chords accompany the evanescent 'And if you wonder' section.

Vega uses an acute sense of taste to illustrate discomfort: 'I am spitting out all the bitterness', and 'It's like drinking gasoline to quench a thirst', which makes this track unique, since so many other songs from her repertoire rest on visual cues.

The game of chess becomes a metaphor for disarming romantic love, as she assigns personalities and feelings of anxiety to the queen and the pawn.

In terms of collaboration, it was likely a challenge for the musicians to follow the rubato tempo. Although there is mention of a confused queen, this character is the polar opposite of the monarch in 'The Queen and the Soldier', which is a crystal-clear story song. Here, the listener faces a potpourri of images, which, while fascinating, feel like a jigsaw puzzle with a handful of missing pieces.

'Neighborhood Girls' (Suzanne Vega)
Addabbo:

Lenny (Kaye) told me, 'You're playing on this one.' I'm not a rock and roll guitar player, but for 'Neighborhood Girls', that was the one where we had the balls to actually bring a drum machine to Folk City. It was really fun, and it was the only time we did it. It was a new sound coming out, what we were doing with her voice; her playing, her voice, and surrounding it with these electric instruments. I never considered Suzanne, a folk singer – I never did.

Addabbo's instincts were right. 'Neighborhood Girls' reveals a shiny new side of Vega's oeuvre. I was entranced by the gorgeous descending bassline Frank Gravis provided, and the incendiary Americana introduction. Vega is exceedingly cool and confident in her delivery against Addabbo's electric and Christian's cutting-edge slide, which anchor this saloon saga. Contrary to the title, the story focuses on one flitting barfly – not a flock.

Addabbo's claim that he's 'not a rock and roll guitar player' doesn't hold water. When he consented to coax the genie out of the bottle, the rhythm section abided – all aced this closer.

The tangible, conversational lyrics dart out at you, similarly to the way a revolving strobe light assaults one's senses in a rock concert arena. Vega was inspired to write the song after she heard a couple of young girls speaking loudly about their personal lives while riding on the New York City subway. Anyone who has taken this transit knows that in such close quarters, it's virtually impossible not to eavesdrop. As such, Vega assigned a fun universality to the chit-chat that the average passenger might have heard, but would have likely ignored.

'Neighborhood Girls' is a relatively innocent and colorful song by today's standards. It's not as rich in detail as Vega's more conventional story songs, but this odd night out at McKinsey's Bar finds its footing with an assured swagger, both instrumentally and vocally. As for the latter, Vega shows great reserve in her use of dynamics.

The verses begin with the tonic, but soon there's an interplay between a sharp eleventh chord and an eleventh. At the chorus, the tension is resolved through the use of simple triads. The simple declarative statement at the chorus: 'She's gone', juxtaposes the complex extensions.

Solitude Standing (1987)

Personnel:
Suzanne Vega: vocals, acoustic guitar
Marc Schulman: electric guitars
Anton Sanko: synthesizers, classical guitar (5)
Michael Visceglia: bass guitar, additional synthesizers (11)
Stephen Ferrera: drums, percussion
Additional personnel:
Shawn Colvin: backing vocals (2)
Mitch Easter: rhythm guitar (9)
Steve Addabbo: guitar (9)
Frank Christian: electric guitar (9)
Jon Gordon: guitar solo (2)
Sue Evans: percussion (7), drums (9)
Label: A&M
Produced at Bearsville (Woodstock), RPM (New York), Carnegie Hill (New York), A&M (Hollywood), Celestial Sound (New York), 1 April 1987 by Steve Addabbo and Lenny Kaye,
Mitch Easter: producer (9)
Ronald K. Fierstein: executive producer
Rod O'Brien: engineer
Shelly Yakus: mixer
Jeffrey Gold: art direction
Melanie Nissen: art direction, design
Paula Bullwinkel: cover photography
Release date: 1 April 1987
Highest chart places: UK (OCC): 2, US Billboard 200: 11, NZL: 1, NOR: 2
Running time: 44:20
Album Art: Vega cups black, gloved hands over either side of her sculptured face. Paula Bullwinkel, who composed the cover photography, took early shots of Kate Moss; later, Morgan Freeman and Mark Ruffalo. After completing Vega's project, she took a portrait shot of Sinead O'Connor for her album cover in 1988. Eventually, Bullwinkel shifted her focus to painting, using the same passion for connecting with the subject.

Vega's work, in part, ushered in an era of observational female singer-songwriters, the likes of: Tracy Chapman, Sarah McLachlan, and Melissa Etheridge, who would release debuts in the next couple of years and also enjoy successful careers. There were thematic parallels.

In 1988, Chapman released 'Behind the Wall,' which she recorded and performed a cappella. It was a fearless undertaking which, like 'Luka', dealt with a taboo topic, namely domestic abuse, and which, like 'Luka', was reenacted in first-person. Like Vega, Chapman had developed a passion for writing prior to reaching her teen years.

'Possession' from McLachlan's 1993 album, *Fumbling Towards Ecstasy,* was based upon chilling letters written by obsessed fans; the stalking of celebrities was a subject publicists historically tried to keep hidden from the public, but when McLachlan deconstructed the perils of fame and allowed the world to see the more morose side of the celebrity, she was doing her contemporaries a favor – it was one thing to admire a performer, and quite another to cross the line into criminality. Celebrities needed to out their stories to potentially protect themselves and others and to spell out the way in which said individuals crossed that line in the sand.

When Etheridge released 'Come to My Window', a breakthrough hit about lesbian love that same year, she also galvanized communities. The song honored another still-taboo topic that was longing to be unleashed and supported by a then-neglected minority and its allies.

But let's backtrack. While Vega would be a major influencer, she still seemed to be wrestling with her own identity when her self-titled album started to receive acclaim. She had every reason to be confident as a recording artist at this juncture. Writing had always been a friend to her in some fashion, whether in the form of stories, lyrics or scribbled entries in a coming-of-age journal. But she had reason to be fearful of the notorious 'sophomore slump', a malady that affects many young artists who first come to the studio to record a debut, with eons of material, but scramble to generate more content the next time around, particularly when facing mounting label pressure. Fortunately, co-producer Addabbo envisioned a light at the end of this tiresome conundrum:

> What was great about the rest of the recording? The A & R people who were involved in the first record left the company. So, in a way, we were left to our own devices to make the rest of the record, which was the best. They weren't pushing anything on us. We just finished the record the way we wanted to. Then, in the end, David Anderle, a producer from A&M, L.A., who was actually the person who rejected us from A&M the very first go-round, came out to see us. In fact, we framed the letter, which stated how Anderle turned us down. Anderle suggested we come down to L.A. and mix the record with Shelly Yakus. That was like the sky opening up because I loved what Yakus did on Tom Petty Records. I'd mixed the first record, but I really didn't have a lot of experience mixing, so having him come in and working with him just made that album gel because I now had someone who really had the confidence to go for it. I never would have spent two-and-a-half days mixing 'Luka', but Yakus said, 'No, we don't have it yet', and kept pushing it. The results were the results. It was incredible.

After the British duo, DNA, consisting of Nick Batt and Neal Slateford, sampled and released a bootleg remix of 'Tom's Diner' in late 1990 called, 'Oh, Susanne!' and sold it in local record stores without A&M's permission,

41

the team dug their heels in. But life would take a strange turn. 'We all hated it. What is this?' Addabbo recalled, 'And all of a sudden, it started taking off in clubs. This is why they made a deal with DNA. They could have sued them. They just bought them out or something. We tried to do a better version and it was ridiculous. But no, just leave it.' Addabbo didn't flinch when asked about his initial reaction but keep in mind, we haven't heard reactions from the rest of the band. 'It's become a bigger song than 'Luka' because everybody knows that song. That song set us up for life more than 'Luka' did,' he added.

Although DNA's version had been unauthorized, Vega's team negotiated to have her sing on the cut, a smart move, as the resultant track became a phenomenal commercial success. The revised electronica track sold three million copies. (The duo would remix Vega's 'Rusted Pipe' a year later, *with* consent. Numerous hip-hop artists, the likes of 2 Pac, Aaliyah, Timbaland and Lil' Kim, would legally sample the song years later).

Major personnel changes ensued: Anton Sanko contributed classical guitar and synthesizer savvy. Down the line, Sanko would assume the role of co-producer. The former NYU student first met Vega when working for her as a session keyboardist. Sanko would eventually win prestigious awards for music for TV and film. Simple Minds and Pink musician Marc Schulman took over lead guitar duties. Bass player Michael Visceglia toured with John Cale (Velvet Underground) and has performed with, among others, Bruce Springsteen and Cyndi Lauper. In 1985, he became a mainstay for Vega in terms of touring and recording purposes. Drummer Stephen Ferrara took on the major role of drummer, Sue Evans stayed on as percussionist and drummer for two tracks.

Vega had achieved an enviable level of notoriety, but fame, unfortunately, came accompanied by a disastrous setback. In 1989, as Vega prepared to headline the UK's iconic Glastonbury Festival, which came to fruition in 1970, and where Elvis Costello, The Wonderstuff, Van Morrison and The Pixies were also scheduled to appear, she received a harrowing death threat. While Vega would have been justified to cancel the date, she forged ahead, so as not to disappoint fans. Statistics show that the attendance leveled off at about 65,000, and while it is true that statistics regarding the actual percentage of strictly Vega fans in attendance may be unknown, the stakes were significantly high that she could have been targeted.

In those days, canceling a concert involved tons of red tape and exhaustive communication. Performing despite the threats was a heroic move, which Vega handled with grace. Wisely, she added a bulletproof vest to her touring wardrobe.

Reviews were complementary. C. Willman, of the *Los Angeles Times*, in 1987, claimed the album was '...full of characters whose shared self-awareness is shaped by their isolation.' *Rolling Stone*'s D. Browne, that same year, compared the album to the debut and summarized it, in part, as 'an

in-your-face-drum mix and more emphasis on synths and electric guitars.'
On 26 December 1987, *Billboard* added: 'True, it doesn't happen often, but intelligent lyrics can sell an album.'

In 1988, Vega discovered remarkable facts about her ancestry: she met her biological father, who, she discovered, played both piano and guitar as well as her paternal grandmother, who also played piano, played drums, sang and toured during the Great Depression.

'Tom's Diner' (Suzanne Vega)
Single releases: UK: 58, IRE: 26

'Tom's Diner' (DNA featuring Suzanne Vega)
Released: 1990, Taste This
Chart places: UK: 2, US: 5

Addabbo:

> We didn't want to include 'Tom's Diner' on that first record, which was probably the first thing that I heard her play. It just seemed like the songs we picked for the first record were for the first record.

Who would have suspected that this simple melody would go gangbusters on the charts, or that the idea would evolve in such an unremarkable setting? Imagine Vega scribbling lyrics over the span of two days, slurping down coffee refills at Tom's Restaurant near Barnard College, and enjoying a ringside view of the passing parade from the window. New York City is loaded with similar establishments – yet Vega cleverly conjured up a lively, breathy storyline complete with urban landmarks and a contagious vibe.

'Tom's Diner', with its blunt orchestra hits, stepwise bassline and Anton Sanko's synth is an American slice of life on steroids. The lyrics reference a deceased American writer (it was written from the male perspective), the horoscope and 'the funnies', but also an archaic church, vis a vis 'the bells of the cathedral', not to mention, a passerby with wet hair hiking up her skirt. This colorful, understated song is constantly being reincarnated on TikTok, among other media sites.

At any number of Vega appearances, audiences often rise to greet her by singing the melody as she graces the stage. Back in the studio, acts have re-imagined their own renditions – there have been numerous international covers of 'Tom's Diner'.

R.E.M., for instance, jumped on the bandwagon in 1991 with *Near Wild Heaven*. Granted, they committed to a tongue-in-cheek rendition, but their interest speaks volumes. For *Radio Bossa* in 2013, jazz ensemble Banda Brasileira foreshadowed the lead vocal with a steamy solo horn. Donna Summer producer, Giorgio Moroder, went for the whole shebang, with an auto-tuned Britney Spears singing over a descending bassline and cutting beats on his 2015 brainchild.

Not to be undone, that same year, the now defunct but once award-winning, all-male, Chicagoland-formed band Fall Out Boy, released 'Centuries' as the lead single from their sixth studio album, *American Beauty/American Psycho*. As opposed to a 'sample', the band used an 'interpolation'; the short, introductory vocal portion was sung by Lolo, while snippets of the melody feature throughout. Vega is included in the list of nine co-writers.

But the song also fueled the imagination of the scientific community when her inarguably clear voice became an unprecedented and cherished prototype. In the article, 'How a Great Song Helped Change the Way We Listen to Music,' published on 21 January 2020, we discover how Vega came to be called the 'Mother of the MP3'.

Audio engineer Karl Heinz Brandenburg, who was working at the AT&T Labs in New Jersey in the late 1980s and 1990s, was seeking a way to 'fine tune my compression algorithm'. Upon hearing 'Tom's Diner', he thought, and later told a magazine: 'I knew it would be impossible to compress this warm a cappella voice.' Ultimately, the team 'repeatedly relied on the song to test the effects of the data compression on the original album mix a cappella version.'

'Luka' (Suzanne Vega)
Single releases: UK: 23, US: 3, NZL: 8, AUS: 5, CAN: 5
A&M executive, Herb Alpert, asked Vega to consider recording the entire album in Spanish. Her step-father had helped with the translation for the bonus CD version from Close-up, but the project never came to pass.

In an interview with the author, Vega acknowledged that she feels protective over 'Luka' and explained the reasons:

> I do watch over it. It depends what people want to use it for. People have used it for domestic violence, PDAs, and I'll allow it for that purpose, but if someone wants to use it for some other reason, I would just suggest that there's probably a better song.

One can sense that protectiveness in Vega's earnest vocals. 'Luka' is one of her most heartfelt story songs, but as a recording, this signature song endured several incarnations. According to Addabbo:

> Suzanne had written this song before the end of the first record but it just didn't seem to be ready or fit for some reason. She had written 'Luka' and the band was on the road playing it live. She was able to get comfortable having more of a rock back beat on it. I was one of the first people to hear that song after she wrote it, and I was just struck with how melodic it was

compared to her other stuff. A lot of Suzanne's stuff is soft of half-singing and half-talking, so when it came time to do 'Luka', we had already done it on the road quite a bit, so we were going for a poppy-rock arrangement, even though the material was what it was – dark. We had done an early version after the pressure of the second record, and well, it was pretty heavy actually, because after we finished the first record and toured the record, and it was time to go into the studio, she really didn't have the songs for the second record. All we had was 'Luka', 'Tom's Diner', and 'Gypsy' and maybe 'Some Journey'. As a primer, we thought, we'd start with 'Luka', 'Tom's Diner' and 'Gypsy'. We actually did those early on, and that's when I used Andy Newmark as a drummer because we'd been working with Sue Evans, who was more of a percussionist drummer... when it came time for the next record, I wanted an earlier alternative version of 'Luka' with Newmark that never got released. It was similar to the one we have; the beat, but not as fleshed out.

Gordon:

Why we decided to do a pop arrangement? I really don't know why. Suzanne was really into The Smiths. They had this dichotomy. Morrissey was singing lyrics about the pathos and tremendous tragedies of his life over the sprightly little tracks that the band was doing. So, it had that kind of disconnect between the musical treatment and content of the lyrics. Suzanne was really into them at that point and maybe some of that sensibility had to do with it. But somehow or other, the decision was made that we were going to do a kind of big rock arrangement of the song. And prior to her recording it for that record, she had done a tour previously, maybe in the summer before she went into pre-production for *Solitude Standing*. Before she went into production for that album, she toured Europe and I was with her there. We were workshopping 'Luka' and breaking it into the repertoire... So, we recorded a version that's very much like what we were doing live, only with Andy Newmark, and very much like what was subsequently recorded with the new lineup. It's sitting in the can somewhere, but I don't know where. That version that came out on *Solitude Standing* was largely based on what we had done live and what we had recorded subsequently.

The subject matter was largely taboo. Vega told J. Moser on 16 November 2011 at *blogs.mccall.com*: Back then, it was still something not really talked about and considered more private, so it was crafted for (the music) and then it was also the simplicity of the lyrics and the actual message.' Vega also revealed to C. Stagoff on 25 August 2021 at *njarts.net*, 'I feel I take risks in my music. I take risks in my lyrics and subject matter. I feel I have my own style.'

In regards to the specific topic at hand, Vega told Stagoff that her tense relationship with her stepfather affected her writing and overall self-expression:

It affected my character and my nature because, as a child, I was constantly watching and trying to figure out what was happening and where I fit into everything and what I was responsible for and what I wasn't responsible for...

In an author interview conducted on 13 March 2012, Vega elaborated on her relationship with her stepfather and how it impacted her writing: '...probably the fact that I was someone else's child influenced it in that I always had a bit of a feeling of being an outsider, and I think that has informed my songwriting.'

Maybe it was, in part, Vega's visceral understanding of hypervigilance that makes the story come across so authentically. Child abuse was certainly not talked about at the time Vega wrote 'Luka', nor was she the first artist to tackle this sensitive subject – Pat Benatar co-wrote 'Hell is for Children' with Neil Giraldo and Roger Capps for her 1980 *Crimes of Passion* album. The band delivered Benatar's third-person exploration with a driving rock beat and pain-inducing electric guitar licks. The team were inspired after reading disturbing articles in *The New York Times*.

Vega and her team, of course, made different decisions about the instrumental portion of this heartbreaking theme – it's light, poppy and danceable.

Conveying the story in first-person with Vega's mellow voice was extremely effective, too, but the song was not entirely a work of fiction. To Siobhan Long at *hotpress.com* on 12 March 2001, Vega said that 'Luka' related to Vega's own experience of contending with abuse. In essence, 'Luka' underscored a topic that begged to be voiced and Vega approached the troubling subject intelligently, by balancing out the heated words with the airy soundscape. At that point in time, performers often had to sugarcoat serious subject matter so that audiences would not feel offended, or guilty, since it was often the case that records wouldn't sell or influence if the artist came on too strong, or inspired action.

Nevertheless, 'Luka' appealed to pop music lovers as well as the socially conscious. Vega's subject is a young, abused boy who lives upstairs. The story feels authentically told, and while the narrative is not based on a real boy, she did know of a boy with that name but is quick to point out to reporters that 'Luka' is an imagined character.

The lyric is simple but pragmatic and moving. Vega parcels out the phrases in short clips, almost like a news anchor, where the who, what and where are immediately discernable. Moreover, Vega's innate ability to sound youthful and innocent propels the story to life.

But underlying that simmering story is Gordon's compelling riff and, across the board, there is that unforgiving beat – 'Luka' hits the mark on so many levels.

But Vega didn't write the song with activist leanings. In the same interview, she explained:

> First of all, when I wrote the song, I had no expectations of having any kind of audience, or a very small one. Child abuse is not something people like to hear about or talk about, so I wrote it because I wanted to write the song, but I wasn't writing it to make a statement – I was writing it to express that point of view. So, I decided to make it as simple as possible and as truthful as possible, just strip away anything that didn't need to be said, and I wanted to do it in the way a child would do it. I think that's what eventually happened; in the three or four verses that I got down there, I managed to get the problem, which is that you have a problem, but you can't say it, but it still exists. In a sense, I'm blaming the neighbor – there is a neighbor involved – Luka is talking to a neighbor so there's that implication that if you hear something... but that doesn't do anything.

Vega's insights bring to light real world issues that continue to this day. The perpetrator hurts others, but so do those that stand by in silence, knowing that hurt has happened.

Since the mid-1980s, many songs in popular culture have tapped into the theme of child abuse: 'Ultraviolence' by Lana Del Ray, 'Wakin' Up' by Lucinda Williams, 'Universal Child' by Annie Lenox, 'The Story of Beauty' by Destiny's Child, 'Take Off Your Shoes' by Sinead O'Connor, 'Slide' by the Dresden Dolls and 'Not to Blame' by Joni Mitchell are just a sampling. In the final analysis, though, it was writers, the likes of Vega and Benatar, that opened the door to substantial healing through story songs. They spearheaded the dissolution of a societal taboo.

The visual appropriation of 'Luka' is well worth mentioning, too. Yonkers, New York actor Jason Cerbone portrayed the seven-year-old 'Luka' character in the related video. He would land the role for the third season production of Giacomo Jackie Aprile Jr. in The Sopranos, a HBO series about members of the Mob and their families.

Finally, one cannot underestimate the breadth of 'Luka' in terms of its appeal to a pantheon of future singer-songwriters. That said, an astute fan on *YouTube* pointed out the parallels between 'Luka' and Regina Spektor's 'Pavlov's Daughter' released in 2001.

In both first-person penned songs, the introductory line begins simply with 'My name is.' The second lines deal with the precise geographic location in the building in which the major subject resides – Spektor's character lives 'downstairs'; 'Luka' lives 'on the second floor.'

On the third line, there are auditory triggers. Luka alerts: 'If you hear something late at night,' while Spektor's character claims to hear the girl taking out the trash. In both cases, something clandestine takes place in real-time.

The next two lines convey a deeper feeling of uneasiness. We are privy to a story with a dire outcome in both cases. Some Spektor fans wonder if she consciously intended her character to be Luka's neighbor. Are the similarities coincidental?

'Luka' placed Vega in a position with her fans that she may not have anticipated, but which she truly took to heart. She was still young herself, but when fans reached out, she felt obliged to reply. She told David Chiu for the article, '30 Years Ago: Solitude Standing Propels Suzanne Vega to Stardom', on 1 April 2017:

> I wrote to every person who wrote to me that year. If I had to give advice, I sometimes would give advice; like 'get professional help' or 'don't stay in that situation'. It was a lot to deal with, and I still get letters.

Singer-songwriter Tori Amos faced a similar challenge when revealing through 'Me and a Gun' and interviews that she'd been a survivor of sexual violence. She also offered emotional support to her fans via educational resources, hotlines and opportunities for discourse.

Sometimes fans want too much from their heroes. Thematic authenticity can lead to an artist being seen as a spokesperson for a cause; it's no wonder that an artist can feel overwhelmed when being asked to assume such a role, despite the best intentions.

'Ironbound/Fancy Poultry' (Suzanne Vega, Anton Sanko)
'Ironbound' came out of the 'woodshedding' experience. Addabbo recalled that the song was 'so beautiful'. Vega set this song in a Portuguese community in New Jersey, and at 6:19, this is the lengthiest album track. It is smartly embellished by Stephen Ferrara's intuitive drumming, Mike Visceglia's crawling bass and co-writer Sanko's surreal effects.

On the surface, the theme centers around a seemingly hardworking female inhabitant at a populated marketplace; we don't find out much about the subject's physical appearance, but then again, Vega muses about 'blood and feathers' and 'breasts and thighs'. The bone-chilling lines are also somewhat ambiguous. Is Vega referring to the actual poultry or how the female subject sees herself, or how she is actually being perceived or treated by others?

The subject walks 'him up to the gate in front of the iron-bound school yard.' As the story develops further, the subject comes across as a very human, struggling single parent. At an especially sobering moment, she 'opens her purse, feels a longing.' Vega gives the impression that the subject is a sympathetic, but somewhat invisible character by society's patriarchal standards, so much so that she is undeserving of an actual name or term of address.

The moniker 'Fancy Poultry' was literally inspired by a pedestrian meat market sign. This ambling, ambient and cinematic instrumental is artfully placed in the sequence. The combination of a fleshed-out story and wordless add-on signifies a clever, compositional turn, one we've not heard before, that allows us to take an empathetic cleansing breath.

'In the Eye' (Suzanne Vega, Marc Schulman)
Addabbo:

> That was the work of keyboard player Anton Sanko and guitarist Mark Schulman. A lot of that was Anton on synthesizer and having the band come up with stuff. That wasn't so much my production as it was letting the band find their way and guiding it. That was a pretty cool track, although I think it might have done better as a single, but I don't think we ever released it as a single. After 'Luka' and the 'Tom's Diner' thing happened a year or two later, 'In the Eye' was in a different direction.

A different direction, indeed. On this suspenseful co-write, the graphic lyrics could promote a thriller trailer. We're shoved against a wall as we confront a possible killer, but unlike the modus operandi of so many other singers, Vega uses breath and precise phrasing to make her point. Never one to scream or resort to cliched vocal gymnastics, Vega instead, relies on intonation and actual content to transport her narrative.

I believe that this song is about confrontation and survival. It's hypothetical but feels like it's being played out in real-time: 'If you were to kill me now right here', Vega states in the first verse, 'I would still look you in the eye'. The event hasn't yet happened, but the narrator warns the perpetrator that if it does, there will be dire consequences.

At the chorus, she repeats: 'I would not run, I would not turn, I would not hide'. She will protect and advocate for herself at all costs.

As Addabbo says, there was a lot of instrumental group involvement, too. The combination of existing and new personnel adds luster; Visceglia's bassline is invincible, Ferrara cultivated an incredible groove, his fills are gratifyingly fierce, and he refuses to shy away from bold exchanges on the track's compelling interludes.

'Night Vision' (Suzanne Vega, Anton Sanko)
'Night Vision' is based on an evocative poem by Frenchman Paul Eluard, a founder of the Surrealist movement. Eluard's text, in turn, was inspired by a painting by Juan Gris and includes descriptions of a simple room with 'a table, a chair and an empty glass'. Finally, we have Vega's retelling, which yielded rich, descriptive thought.

On YouTube, Vega reveals that 'the first verse and little bits in the middle' are from the poem and 'the rest is about trying to help someone see in the darkness, but not in the literal sense.'

'By day give thanks, by night be wary,' the song begins, based on the poem's first line. The evolution of the theme is exciting. After Vega ascribes an intonational personality to the objects in the room, she guides us through a construct of devout companionship and love.

'Night Vision' has a daring harmonic structure. At the bridge, especially, Vega ushers in sweeping chromatic changes. Her spare, but acute phrases cultivate a sense of untainted humanity. Repetitive droning in the instrumental portion mirrors Philip Glass minimalism. Addabbo also recalled: 'With the classical guitar (played by Mark), this song was a real contrast to the other tracks.'

'Solitude Standing' (Suzanne Vega, Anton Sanko, Mark Schulman, Michael Visceglia, Stephen Ferrera)
Single releases: UK: 79, US: 94, US Main: 43
The cinematic 'Solitude Standing' also came out of that same 'woodshedding' experience at Vega's Cape Cod house. Addabbo remembered how the signature song originated:

It was the band writing a song out of segments that Suzanne was writing. There are not a lot of lyrics to that song. Steve Ferrara came up with that great beat. Anton came up with that amazing super side. That was really the band putting together the song. Suzanne could play it by herself; the guitar part was in there, but there wasn't a lot of writing in that song. She kind of came up with the verse.

Sanko's escalating, exhilarating keyboard run extends to and throughout the outro. Visceglia is unstoppable; Schulman goes full tilt in this study of exceptional teamwork.

'Solitude Standing' required the collaboration of five songwriters and the end result speaks highly of their combined efforts. At its core, 'Solitude' is presented as a peace-loving, physical being. In the first verse, 'she stands by the window' and approaches the narrator with, what appears to be hesitation, or a simple respectfulness for the other's personal space.

In the second verse, she has inched further along, and 'she stands in the doorway.' The narrator is moved by 'her black silhouette, long cool stare and her silence.' 'Solitude' offers her extended palm, 'split with a flower with a flame.' At this point, I can imagine Marcel Marceau, or another talented mime artist, portraying this mysterious, but caring character. The well-positioned use of alliteration is also appealing.

The ghost-like imagery and sonic jambalaya together create a high-octane performance. The related video directed by Jonathan Demme pooled together key human senses: through the lens, Demme conveyed the tensions already inherent in the sound.

Demme was an excellent choice. He had directed powerful films, such as *Swimming to Cambodia*, as well as concert films and videos, including *Stop Making Sense* (1984), a documentary about The Talking Heads. In 1998, he directed a documentary about British singer-songwriter Robyn Hitchcock.

'Calypso' (Suzanne Vega)
To me, Vega's voice sounded markedly different on this track. According to Addabbo: 'It could just be the way we treated her voice. It was an older song, and in juxtaposition to the new stuff, it might be her approach to singing the song, too.'

Vega gleaned inspiration from Homer's Odyssey for 'Calypso'. She assumes the voice of the sea nymph who saves the drowning Ulysses and partners with him for seven years until Hermes calls him home. Vega, haunted by Calypso's post-mortem, pondered over Calypso's reaction. Was Calypso manipulated into sending Ulysses home? Was she quietly heroic?

In full-blown feminist mode and with allusions, Vega reimagines the myth. Amid celestial sonics and angelic harmonies, 'Calypso' divulges her side without standing on ceremony. 'I let him go,' she declares, without assigning blame, while leaving her dignity intact. 'In the day he sails away,' she narrates in a perfunctory manner. After a rush of commentary, she ultimately contends with her fate through either suicide, or extreme grief, depending on the source: The *Fabulae* (Hyginus) claims Calypso committed suicide, but because she was immortal, other sources disagree.

In an author interview from 2012, Vega examines inspirations:

It was my first year in college and I was taking this Humanities course, and one of the first things we had to read was Homer's 'The Odyssey' and I remember being struck by the whole situation. I had a boyfriend at the time that would call me 'Circe' as a nickname to annoy me, and it did annoy me. And I don't feel like Circe. I'm not turning anybody into swine. If I'm like any goddess around here, I suppose, I'm more like Calypso, because he (Ulysses) was always leaving. So, that's what goaded me into writing the song. She nurtured him. He landed there shipwrecked and all he could think about was his wife back home. So, I've had people write to me and say, 'So what about Penelope?' That's not as interesting to me as Calypso. And it would be interesting to write a song from 'Circe's' point of view, too. What is her motivation?

In an author interview from 19 June 2015, Vega explained that she admired Calypso 'for her resilience and strength,' and because 'she offers him (Odysseus) her immortality.' He says, 'No thank you. I need to go home. I need to be a human and suffer my human life.' I like her. I have a lot of sympathy for her.' Then, Vega saw a painting from 1670 of Calypso and broadened her perspective:

She actually seems to be in the middle of this wild, debauched orgy with Odysseus and Hermes, and all these cherubs frolicking and Gods and Goddesses watching down and she's hardly got any clothes on and she's in the arms of Odysseus and she's looking right into the audience. It's a very modern perspective and I was so struck by this because I always thought of her as so stoic and mature about the whole thing. She helps him build the ship and gives him food, but in this picture, it's really like sex, drugs and rock 'n' roll.

'Language' (Suzanne Vega, Michael Visceglia)
Addabbo implied that Vega had suffered from writer's block:

So, what came out was a bit more minimalist than before. If you compare 'Language' with 'Luka' and 'Tom's Diner', which had very strong melodies, a lot of this other stuff didn't necessarily have the melodies, but it was, you might say, more Reed influenced, or Glass influenced. Anton was into that type of music, too, the more modern composers, and that started to leak in with 'Language'. That's a beautiful lyric.

'If language were liquid it would be rushing in...' is Vega's complex opening line. This appears to be a song about our overdependence on this one sense at the expense of all other senses. She deconstructs this obsession in the second verse: these words 'don't move fast enough to catch the blur in the brain.'

After the hypotheticals, she reaches out to another person she'd like to meet. She inhabits a physical space, where 'we'll sit in the silence,' but juxtaposes her monologue with negative comments about words she uttered earlier: 'they don't move fast enough...'

She then comes back with more resolve: 'I won't use words again,' and in the final verse, she repeats what she said initially. One can feel the frustration that Suzanne Vega, the once-reserved toddler, might have felt, when life was charging ahead at a rapid pace, and her childlike voice could barely express what may have been bottled up for too long.

In an interview with the author, Vega explained that 'Language' was written from her own point-of-view based on actual life experience. She didn't speak until she was about two-and-a-half, which worried her mother greatly: 'She said she was relieved when I started to read when I was about three because before that they thought I was a little slow in the head.'

Was she simply absorbing all the sights and sounds around her? Linguistics experts often stress the importance of acquiring receptive language skills prior to attempting speech.

Yes, there was a lot to see and those were the years when we had moved from California to New York, so there was a lot to take in. There was a lot going on and I probably didn't have a lot to say, so anyway, I've always found language to be, especially in emotional moments, very difficult, something that I have to sit and work with.

'Language' has insightful, meaningful content, but is trumped by heavy competition in this diverse collection. Of course, because the current generation often hunts and pecks through isolated songs on the net, sequencing is probably not an issue.

'Gypsy' (Suzanne Vega)
Single release UK: 77

Addabbo:

> We almost didn't include 'Gypsy' because it was too folky, but on the second record, it fit in as a very different texture – it had an Americana feel. Suzanne wrote that when she was about seventeen and had a camp counselor crush. In fact, that was the oldest song on the record. That was another one in which the label was trying to push people on us: 'Let's bring this in. Let's bring that in. They brought Mitch Easter in to co-produce on that song, but that was from the early sessions, that first go-round. I played guitar on 'Gypsy'. That was another one that Mitch Easter made me play. He said, 'No, you do it.' (Easter produced REM's early albums from 1981-1984 and was the frontman of Let's Active). But that was the great thing about working with Suzanne. The quieter she got, the more intense she got, which was something she did very well live, too. She had a very good stage presence and that translated into the studio.

I wondered whether Addabbo ever considered double-tracking Vega's voice to create a stronger sound when the lyric demanded it: 'What's great about her voice is the edges on the sound of her voice, and if you double track it, it creates something else, but it loses the intimacy a little bit, at least for her.'

In an interview with the author in 2012, Vega said: 'Gypsy was a sincere love song to a man I was involved with. I still feel myself to be the narrator of that song.'

'Gypsy' stands in deep contrast to the thematic torpedo 'Luka'. As Addabbo points out, Vega wrote the song as a teenager; as a counselor in upstate New York, when she was only eighteen. Her fresh, wide-eyed infatuation shines through in the lyric and the breezy acoustic chord changes. She will revisit this whirlwind relationship on 'In Liverpool' from the 1992 album, *99.9F*.

'Gypsy' has been pervasive in popular culture and is mentioned as being part of Charlie, the main character's mixtape in the book, *The Perks of Being a Wallflower* by Stephen Chbosky.

'Wooden Horse (Casper Hauser's Song)' (Vega, Visceglia, Sanko, Schulman, Ferrera)
Released on *Retrospective* and *Solitude Standing*, Vega took a deep dive into the phenomenon of isolation and its effect on the development of the human psyche. The curious and sobering prose is based on the true story of a German youth raised in solitary confinement.

Vega informs us of her subject's vulnerability in the first verse, where she relays that the subject comes out of the darkness, 'holding one thing, a small white wooden horse, I'd been holding inside.' The young boy's tale unfolds as a story within a story, and as a listener, I feel very much a part of the scene. It's as if I'm loosening up the top of a large Russian matryoshka doll and, feeling anxious to reach the tiniest one, I rummage through the others in a tizzy, but then stop to appreciate the one I've just unpacked, acknowledging that this one is just as real and valid as the next. 'Wooden Horse' deserves a lot of listens, as each verse builds on the previous one and every verse is laden with emotion and keen insight.

Moreover, the track is markedly percussive; the strumming is aggressive and the bassline grumbles in kind. Lines such as 'What was wood became alive,' and 'In the night, the walls disappeared, in the day they returned,' lead us to understand the hell the child is enduring. Vega's insights into this bleak historical event involving Hauser make the tiniest detail haunting.

It's notable that the song was co-written by five musicians, including Vega, which I believe confirms her willingness to collaborate and remain open to new ideas.

'Tom's Diner (reprise)' (Suzanne Vega)
Addabbo:

> That was us horsing around in rehearsal. Once we were ready to do the rest of the album, we went up to Bearsville Studios in New York. And it's one of those things where, maybe Anton starts playing a melody and then the bass part starts showing up, and all of a sudden we had this reprise version. It was fun to do and we didn't take it too seriously. It kind of emerged out of the guy's playing. The *a cappella* version was pretty gutsy, I think.

'Gutsy' and fun. The band got impressive mileage out of this simple tune which so neatly sandwiches other tracks.

Remarkably, Vega wasn't married to the idea of 'Tom's Diner' being set in New York, even though her references earmarked that locale. Her motivation, in fact, was to create a mood; the physical setting was incidental. In an interview with the author on 13 March 2012, Vega discussed 'Tom's Diner' and cleared up related misconceptions:

> It probably could be anywhere – the sense of alienation. A diner is a funny thing. It's kind of a midpoint between being home and being out in the street. You can either feel a sense of community there with other people or you could feel alienated, so it probably could have taken place any place where there is a diner.

Days of Open Hand (1990)

Personnel:
Suzanne Vega: vocals, acoustic guitar (1, 2, 4, 6, 9), backing vocals (1, 2, 4, 7, 11), Fairlight synthesizer on 'Rusted Pipe' and 'Big Space)
Anton Sanko: guitar, Hammond C3 organ, tiple, Sequential V.s., Dx711, Voyetra 8, Fairlight synthesizers, Akai S-1000 sampler, programming; string arrangement on 'Institution Green.'
Shawn Colvin: backing vocals (2, 4)
Marc Schulman: E-bow on 'Institution Green' and 'Predictions,' electric guitar (1-5, 9, 11), tiple guitar (1, 6, 8, 11), twelve-string electric guitar on 'Book of Dreams,' bouzouki on 'Big Space'
Michael Visceglia: five-string bass (1-4, 6), fretless bass (5, 9, 11)
Erik Sanko: fretless bass on 'Room off the Street,'
Percy Jones: fretless bass on 'Predictions'
John Linnell: accordion on 'Tired of Sleeping'
Richard Horowitz: ney on 'Room off The Street'
Hearn Gadbois: dumbek
Michael Blair: marimba on 'Rusted Pipe,' metal percussion and tambourine on 'Men in a War' and 'Book of Dreams,' percussion on 'Institution Green,' shaker in 'Room off the Street,' hand drum and shaker on 'Pilgrimage'
Philip Glass: string arrangement on 'Fifty-Fifty Chance'
Maria Kitsopoulos: cello on 'Institution Green'
Fred Zlotkin: cello on 'Fifty-Fifty Chance'
Sandra Park: first violin on 'Institution Green'
Barry Finclair: violin solo on 'Fifty-Fifty Chance'
Hae Young Ham: violin on 'Institution Green'
Timothy Baker: violin on 'Fifty-Fifty Chance
Rebecca Young: viola on 'Institution Green'
Alfred Brown: viola on 'Fifty-Fifty Chance'
Label: A&M
Produced by Anton Sanko and Suzanne Vega on 10 April 1990 at Skyline Studios, New York City, RPM Studios, New York City, The Living Room, New York City
Bob Ludwig: mastering
Hugh Padgham: mixing
Pat McCarthy: engineer
Pat Dillett: assistant engineer
Geoff Keehn: engineer
Jeff Lippay: assistant engineer
Jon Goldberger: assistant engineer
Kurt Munkasci: string engineer
Release date: 10 April 1990
Highest chart places: UK (OCC): 7, US Billboard 200: 50
Running time: 45:51

Album Art: Now out-of-print in the US, the album won a Grammy for Best Recording Package in 1991. The letters of Vega's name are spelled out and inserted inside white boxes In a stylized image that lies below.

As for Vega, she is positioned inside a box. Her hair is cropped short and her face is positioned at a three-quarter angle – she glances to the side. Her oversized right-hand beckons, as if to offer the viewer unconditional acceptance.

At her left, a sculptured hand holds a cigarette. A tiny book lies beneath, and to the side sits a spinner. The abstract cover hints at the contents, in contrast to previous albums, casting asunder Vega's folk image, painting a portrait of an artist existing between realms.

Vega was up against a maelstrom of male bands in April of 1990. The debut, *39/Smooth*, by Green Day, in part, examined the lighter side of punk. Fugazi's *Repeater* radiated anger with tightly crafted, concise rants. When recording *The Good Son*, Nick Cave & The Bad Seeds made no bones about containing the dark subject matter. Nirvana would drastically change the era's sonic landscape with *Nevermind* in the fall of 1991. Sinead O'Connor's melodic 'Nothing Compares 2 U' galvanized the charts from late April to mid-May, securing the number one spot on the *Billboard* Hot 100. Madonna and Wilson Phillips were not far behind. Among these acts, Vega was unique; trying to compete with the motley male 'grunge' movement coming out of Seattle would have been inauthentic, of course, but could she continue to stay in vogue during this obvious musical shift?

After two years of tour support for *Solitude Standing*, Vega was under pressure to conceptualize and orchestrate her own content. She also had to make a series of executive decisions regarding personnel.

To that end, Vega would enlist an impressive series of co-producers over the course of her studio recording career. For *Days of Open Hand*, she assigned these tasks to Anton Sanko, a multi-instrumentalist and a known quantity on her previous work, who would produce scores for *Ouija, Jessabelle* and *Visions* the following year.

Arrangements received royal treatment by virtue of lush strings, bouzouki, state-of-the-art synthesizers and assorted bass instruments – the fretless bass featuring prominently. Michael Visceglia and Mark Schulman were at the ready – the former musician had been bassist on 1987's *Solitude Standing* and *Live at The Royal Albert Hall* that same year. Schulman would go on to perform with Foreigner and Simple Minds. Composer Philip Glass arranged violins, viola and cello on 'Fifty-Fifty Chance'. With talented, repeat instrumentalists, enviable guests and an award-winning producer, what could go wrong?

On the surface, the sky was the limit. Vega had achieved success with her self-titled debut and had thrived when others crashed and burned during the perilous sophomore slump. Before her now, though, stood a blank canvas awaiting a gouache of infinite color; this was not an insurmountable task, but she was certainly facing a new set of issues.

In an interview with the author on 13 March 2012, Vega revealed:

Anton and I were living together and working on the album together, and I just had this huge success with *Solitude Standing*. There was a lot of pressure, and I just found that I didn't want to be there. A lot of times I would just go out for a walk or do anything just to avoid doing my vocals and there was no other place to go. I decided after that I was never going to work out of my house again. I just thought, no, no, no, and when I listen back to it, I hear the strain that we were under. The songs were good, but I think the production was stilted in some way, not through any fault of our own – it was just the stress of the situation.

Reviews were mixed: G. Sandow, for *ew.com* on 20 April 1990, wrote favorably of the lyrics: 'Vega's flickering play of meaning, sound and rhythm is far beyond ordinary.' But Sandow was lackluster when critiquing the instrumental portion: '...even if we sometimes catch a hint of such ethnic instruments as the dumbek and tiple – (they) smell not much different from the bright and sensitive orchestration apt to accompany other folkish singer-songwriters.'

On the other hand, Sandow specifically praised the work of Philip Glass, claiming that the composer's style here was 'much more flowing than his usual romantic minimalism.' (Glass's experimental music, which was frequently based on hypnotic, repetitive sound fragments and arpeggios became known as 'minimalism', a term that the composer would decry as limiting).

Sandow added that Glass 'outdoes' Vega 'in both the strength and detail of the feeling he conveys.' But to be fair, the critique reads like an apples-to-oranges argument: Vega is a poet who also writes music and Glass is a composer. How can they be equally appraised?

Glass, a Julliard-trained composer who became entranced by world music, had been sought after by multiple pop/rock artists, including David Bowie, Mick Jagger, Brian Eno and Talking Heads. Swirling cinematic scores, such as *Mishima: A Life in Four Chapters* and *The Hour* inspired dialogue as much as the movies themselves.

Like Vega, Glass was heavily influenced by the words of Leonard Cohen, but he also admired Vega's poetic gifts and contacted her for inclusion in the 1986 *Songs From Liquid Days*, a musical hybrid based on text. (Paul Simon, David Byrne and Laurie Anderson also contributed). Vega was responsible for 'Lightning' and 'Freezing' (more on that later).

In S. Holden's *The New York Times* review on 20 April 1996, the critic singled out Vega's contribution: 'Miss Vega freezes hot emotions in miniature, precisely detailed still-lives.'

Vega veered away from her folksy reputation for *Days of Open Hand*, and in the process, wove in alluring world music and contemporary beats.

Cognitively, many songs serve as a paean to Socratic thought, where Vega posits more questions than answers, thereby creating a sense of wonderment. Moreover, there's room in this realm for the reader to interact; to bring one's own experiences into the fold.

In interviews, Vega has talked about linking the past to the present, so as with her previous work, time remains a crucial component. Curiously, the explanation for the title is less complex than it appears. While Vega can go for abstractions, this image is fairly straightforward and visceral. She likens the phrase to reaching out one's hand when presented with a wild animal, allowing time for that being to settle down, and finally, establishing a united front.

Vega set the bar high when including artists such as Glass – when a pop artist borrows from the classical world, judgments inherently arise, but I don't believe Vega compromised artistically or philosophically. In fact, I believe fans had an opportunity to watch her transform and take flight, and although *Days of Open Hand* didn't bear the fruit of the signature hits of an earlier time, as an ambitious co-producer, Vega displayed tremendous growth and a raise-your-glass attitude towards collaboration. These traits facilitated more versatility behind the glass.

'Tired of Sleeping' (Suzanne Vega)
Single releases: AUS: 145

Vega faces an intense time: nightmares and interrupted rest torment her, but she searches inwardly and ultimately finds peace through the artistic process. 'Oh, mom, I wonder when I'll be waking,' she asks rhetorically, not expecting a logical answer. Vega's dirge-like melody and hushed yearnings rise above an assault of ringing guitars. A Celtic instrumental interlude precedes more melancholic lyrics, although Vega's voice retains a 'summer of love' innocence. The guests bleed in beautiful touches: John Linnell's sad accordion mirrors the tedium and angst possibly endured by this reluctant night owl. The shift between major and minor tonalities creates a synergetic, see-saw effect.

The poetic elements are stark, yet revealing, too. 'The bird on the string is hanging' is the most cryptic line. Less shocking, but equally heartbreaking is: 'she's fighting for her small life.'

'Men in a War' (Suzanne Vega)

Vega's surreal lyrics address the life of the soldier, who runs the risk of losing limbs and 'a piece of your eyesight.' Moreover, 'Men in a War' is a troubling lyrical think-piece about emotional loss and overwhelming grief.

Similar to 'Luka', a dark topic is cushioned by a glitzy pop arrangement. Strip away the grim content and you'll find quite a crowd-pleasing ditty. Kudos to Shawn Colvin for her bright backing vocals, and Schulman and Visceglia's vigilant footprints. Michael Blair's metal percussion infuses an infectious Caribbean element. The drum fills and vocal call and response come together harmoniously.

Vega often leaves a clean slate available to her listeners; a space where they can assert their own views or envision a wider application. As such, I see 'Men in a War' as being a discourse on universal human bravery, frailty and recovery.

'Rusted Pipe' (lyrics: Suzanne Vega, music: Anton Sanko)
Blair's dancing marimba procures a sparkling counter-rhythm to the alluring vocals. Through the textual onomatopoeia, the struggling water takes on a vivid persona, magnified by the vivid use of kinesthetic verbs: 'gurgle', 'mutter', 'hiss' and 'stutter'.

The double-tracking production of Vega's voice and the bubbling harmonies are unforgettable. The gothic Hammond-C3 trails Vega's voice faithfully, without competing for space, but the shrieking guitar solo, while brief, also warrants a shout-out.

'Book of Dreams' (lyrics: Suzanne Vega, music: Anton Sanko)
Single releases: UK: 66, US Modern: 8, US Main: 47
'Book of Dreams' is a dazzling example of pop splendor; a bright spin on a record awash in somewhat solemn subjects. I enjoyed the light, airy backup vocals, abstract imagery and the uncompromising backbeat, courtesy of Frank Vilardi.

Vega got slammed a lot for this smooth, contagious track. After all, she'd gone for the jugular vein on the first couple of albums, and also on *Days of Open Hand*. She'd become the poster child, of sorts, for the socially conscious. That said, we don't always allow our philosophers to let their hair down, and often demonize those that try. But I see 'Book of Dreams' as a cool distractor from the album's pensive themes.

Andrew Doucette, who also took charge of a music video for Amy Grant in 2004, directed the light-hearted video, where imagination takes root in roulette wheels and Vega's Kriegsmarine naval uniform. The sunny video won a Grammy for art production.

'Institution Green' (lyrics; Suzanne Vega, music: Anton Sanko)
The lengthiest song on the album at 6:15, 'Institution Green' revolves around the disheartening plight of mentally ill patients. Here, they get heard, amid Michael Blair's clawing, industrial digs and an apocalyptic Jah Wobble-type bass line. By the end of the song, it's conceivable that Vega sees us all as victims of institutions, in whatever forms that may take: exhausted people 'waiting to be seen'.

The physical imagery suggests that this institution is a worn-down, soulless 'public place'. Simultaneously, Vega inserts her vision of how human beings typically react in a similarly bleak environment. A sense of emotional weariness and anonymity follow. Patients feel invisible in a room devoid of warmth or comfort. We can all relate.

The word 'green' is not incidental. Vega had a bee in her bonnet about the actual color and the fact that it appears in so many grammar schools and waiting rooms in doctors' offices. It's not a color that easily fades into the background and it is not generally associated with cheerful thoughts. But Vega has an axe to grind with the bureaucratic system and that frustration comes through sonically and psychologically.

'Those Whole Girls (Run in Grace)' (Suzanne Vega)
'Those whole girls run in packs...' But before we imagine their wild escapade, we're accosted by a blister of hypnotic electronics – the Akai S-1000 and Sanko's Fairlight – which, after a series of cliffhanger measures that drift off, are replaced with acoustic guitar.

This ethereal song leaves an imprint similar to the way a frigid blast of wintry air leaves goosebumps on exposed skin. The sitting-on-the-edge tension reminded me of the title song of Patti Smith's 1975 epic, *Horses*.

The depth of emotion lies in the actual movement, not in the actual lyrics, which are, in comparison to the other tracks, quite benign. In contrast to many of the other tracks, the song ends with a positive phrase: 'run in grace.'

'Room off the Street' (lyrics: Suzanne Vega, music: Anton Sanko)
Originally entitled 'Cuba,' this acted-out story song is flush with vivid detail. There's 'a woman who's drinking and dress is so tight you can see every breath that she takes.' The male character first appears on a poster with a raised fist. Between the hand claps, goblet drum, the ney (an ancient, end-blown flute traditionally used in Persian, Turkish and Arabic music) and Vega's backing vocals, a plethora of sonics abound, over which the couple spar.

The revolutionaries interface with intense passion, as they explore their allegiance and fight for freedom. Musically, the intense conversation comes across over moments of silence and clanking rhythms. Vega's singsong, wordless ending doesn't resolve the conflict, but it does give us time to ponder their vision.

'Big Space' (lyrics: Suzanne Vega, music: Anton Sanko)
'Big Space' invites major introspection; there is a lot of exciting prose to examine in the droning verses. Over the swell of a Fairlight synthesizer, considered to be a pioneering workstation in the 1980s, and assertive guitar, the exploration swells in complexity, with Vega's subtle phrasing hinting that something more ominous is about to occur.

But keep in mind the title here: 'Big Space', in which the Fairlight plays a dominant, masculine role. Vega and the team created a brand-new world for themselves and their fans on this progressive album, although they certainly weren't the first to fidget with the Fairlight.

Kate Bush was also enamored with the instrumental effects. The British singer used the efficient instrument to spice up 1980's 'Babooshka'. At the end of her signature song, you can hear the Fairlight replicating the disturbing sound of glass being shattered in real-time.

Frankie Goes to Hollywood used the machine on 'Relax' in 1983. Peter Gabriel, who owned the first Fairlight in the UK, made use of its effects generously, too, in major, subsequent works.

'Between the pen and the paperwork, there must be a passion in the language,' Vega proclaims. As we've seen on her previous albums, words mean a great deal to her, and she's not prone to spelling things out, but she's also not timid about parsing out hypotheticals.

The bridge is less definitive, surreal and harmonically complex. Musically, we're meta-versed through a series of mystical undercurrents. But despite the electronic preoccupation, Vega's vocals remain upfront and expressive.

'Predictions' (Suzanne Vega)

Vega's pointed, spoken-word production relies on a constantly moving, ambient, instrumental base, which shimmers like a flash of lightning once her turn has been taken. Vega relays these poetry clips in a matter-of-fact tone, and, as the title suggests, these images foretell pragmatic and imaginative ways of anticipating the future: 'By numbers. By mirrors. By water...'

Michael Blair on percussion, holds no prisoners. Welsh Percy Jones of Brand X, establishes a dirge-like electric bassline that upholds the surrealistic, explosive soundscape so reminiscent of The Beatles' *Sgt. Pepper*. Co-produced by Sanko and Vega, each mines an area of expertise: Sanko with ethereal ambience and Vega with impressive intonation and hypnotic acoustic.

'Fifty-Fifty Chance' (Suzanne Vega)

On this bittersweet Philip Glass string arrangement, Barry Finclair breaks the heart with his dramatic violin solo. He had played with Cleo Laine on *Cleo Laine Sings Sondheim* in 1987. In the year that he recorded with Vega, he played violin with Glass and Ravi Shankar on *Passages*.

'Fifty-Fifty Chance' is a sorrowful song about a suicidal patient. Glass's pulsating arrangement is gripping. However, I was amazed that the team only kept this arrangement going for a mysteriously mere 2:36. It is the shortest track, for some reason, and although the story was succinct in a positive sense, I yearned for the instrumentals to be carried out in full capacity, or at least vis a vis a Seventy-Thirty Chance? It's gorgeous, but I felt short-changed.

'Pilgrimage' (lyrics: Suzanne Vega, music: Anton Sanko)

After an extended, dreamy electronic introduction, Vega sets the stage for a creative string of other-worldly harmonies and cryptic observations. The lyrics in the first verse are hard-hitting and lucid: 'This life is burning, turning to ash as it hits the air.'

61

Then, in the second verse, Vega's tone remains relatively the same, but the electronic sounds and percussive elements build force, creating an almost competitive, conversational line.

It's an observation of an unpredictable world, which Vega unravels with relatable revelations. At first, as the omnipotent narrator, she keeps a cool distance, but then she becomes a guiding force, a ray of enlightenment, perhaps even a savior, as she veers from narrator to friend with the lines: 'I'm coming to you. I'll be there in time.' Vega's own backing harmonies are subtle and slightly dissonant, which adds to the mystique.

The repetition acts as a soothing balm. When we are unsure, we need that calming voice of the elder, or even the wise acquaintance who reassures us. We don't need to know exactly when we'll be rescued, just that we will. Her assurance is the payoff: 'I'll be there in time.'

This subject matter represents a roundabout from Vega's early works. The slick, urban songwriter, prone to glorifying her gritty city, and zeroing in on its inhabitants, begins an exploration of the metaphysical: the imagined afterlife, with equal veracity. Vega told *unmask.us*:

What really occurred to me writing 'Pilgrimage' was that your life comes back again, not necessarily as a person or animal but more in a scientific way. I will not be myself in the future, but I'll be present to some degree, even if my body goes back into the earth and is dispersed.

99.9F (Ninety-Nine Point Nine Fahrenheit Degrees) (1992)

Personnel:
Suzanne Vega: vocals, acoustic guitar
Mitchell Froom: keyboards, string arrangement (12)
Tchad Blake: electric guitar (3, 4, 6, 10)
David Hidalgo: electric guitar (1, 2, 3, 4, 7, 8, 11)
Bruce Thomas: bass guitar
Jerry Marotta: drums, percussion
Additional personnel:
Richard Pleasance: electric guitar (1, 3, 10)
Michael Visceglia: fretless bass guitar (5)
Richard Thompson: guitar solo (11)
Greg Smith: baritone saxophone (8, 11)
Jerry Scheff: double bass (6, 12)
Marc Schulman: bouzouki (5)
Sid Page: first violin (12)
Joel Derouin: second violin (12)
Maria Newman: viola (12)
Larry Corbett: cello (12)
Suzie Katayama: copyist (12)
Label: A&M
Produced: Mitchell Froom at Dreamland (Bearsville, New York), The Sound Factory (Los Angeles), The Magic Shop (New York City) on 8 September 1992
Ronald K. Fierstein: executive producer
Tchad Blake: engineer, mixing
Len Peltier: art direction
Release date: 8 September 1992
Highest chart places: UK (OCC): 20, US Billboard 200: 86
Running time: 37:20
Related singles: '99.9F', UK singles: 46, US Alternative Songs: 13, 'Blood Makes Noise', UK Singles: 60, US Alternative Songs: 1, 'In Liverpool', UK Singles: 52, 1992, 'When Heroes Go Down', UK Singles: 58, 1993
Album Art: Although Vega's hand loosely covers her nose and mouth, it's obvious that she is hiding an impish grin. Her face is surrounded by exaggerated flames of orange and yellow hair.

After deciding against self-production, Vega interviewed three different producers for this new project. With *Days of Open Hand* receiving mixed reviews, she had to shake the trees. Mitchell Froom, who had worked alongside Crowded House, the L.A.-based Los Lobos and Elvis Costello, among others, passed the litmus test. Froom's pitch included a detailed timeline and a blueprint of exhilarating sonic effects.

Froom, a full-spectrum professional, is not only a producer but a seasoned musician. In 1994, he began performing with Latin Playboys, a band originally intended to be a Los Lobos side-project but became a full-blown, dynamic act, specializing in, but not limited to, Tex-Mex, experimental rock, Latin rock and avant-garde. They disbanded in 1999.

That band included passionate multi-instrumentalist David Hidalgo and versatile percussionist and guitarist Louie Perez, founding Los Lobos members. The East L.A. band came to fame with their cover of Ritchie Valens's 'La Bamba' for the movie released in 1987 of the same name.

Los Lobos was a rare bird. The ensemble switched effortlessly between Tex-Mex and traditional Mexican music. Their discography included cumbia, boleros and nortenos, as well as R&B, zydeco, blues, country and classic rock. Acclaimed for adding counter-rhythms to otherwise ordinary arrangements, Hidalgo had much to offer.

Texan Tchad Blake was Froom's right-hand accomplice in audio engineering; Blake's tool kit involved using a binaural microphone system that had the capacity to create a 3D sound.

Blake's CV boasted work with The Pretenders, Tom Waits, The Black Keys, Sheryl Crow and Tracy Chapman. He would eventually go on to win a Grammy Award for Best Engineered Album, Non-Classical for Vega's 2007 *Beauty & Crime*.

Without a doubt, Froom's association with these band members put him in good stead; when assembling the studio team, he pooled talent from the bands he knew best, and with the addition of other successful sidemen, talent was limitless. Bassist Bruce Thomas was a longstanding member of Elvis Costello and The Attractions. Melodic, larger-than-life bassist Jerry Scheff was acclaimed for working with Elvis Presley. Richard Thompson, a versatile British guitarist, admired for his intricate fingerstyle technique, had made a name for himself with the folksy Fairport Convention before going solo.

But even if Vega had known little about Froom's background, or that of his colleagues, Froom may have been in the running. The emotional chemistry was right. When Vega queried Froom about his studio approach, he offered frank, incremental suggestions that correlated with her open-minded vision. To her credit, Vega was anxious and willing to reinvent herself by experimenting with unique textures, beats and a virtual overhaul of bright new sounds.

Most importantly, Vega and Froom's meeting of the minds preceded production deadlines, so by the time the team settled in behind the glass, Froom had had ample time to sketch out ideas and present them to Vega in a relatable, linear manner. He had certainly done his homework as a producer, but as a colleague, he also demonstrated sensitivity to Vega's artistic spirit.

In a *Fresh Air Archive* from 10 November 2016, moderated by long-term broadcaster Terry Gross, Froom was asked about his role in *99.9F*. Froom explained why he thought that Vega had chosen him to produce the project:

Above: From a Chicago hotel room in 1987, Vega's gaze recalls the line, 'I am watching you', from 'Small Blue Thing'. (*Paul Natkin*)

Below: Bedecked with bling, Vega sings a soulful ballad at S.P.A.C.E. in Evanston, Illinois in 2013. (*Philamonjaro*)

Left: Original music from Vega's self-titled debut continues to garner audience requests. The album was platinum certified in the UK. (*A&M*)

Right: Debut single, 'Marlene on the Wall', inspired by actor Marlene Dietrich, and re-released in 1986, was Vega's first Top 40 UK hit. (*A&M*)

Left: Vega mined Greek mythology and poetry for her US platinum-certified sophomore album. 'Tom's Diner' inspired an MP3 software prototype. (*A&M*)

Right: Vega's zeal for dance shines through in this black-and-white still, but 'the music behind the wild beat' gradually won over. (*A&M*)

Left: Co-written by Vega and Steve Addabbo, 'Left of Centre' reached great heights after appearing in the *Pretty in Pink* (1986) soundtrack. (*A&M*)

Right: Co-produced by Vega and Anton Sanko, 1990's *Days of Open Hand* was a precursor to Vega's experimental studio albums. (*A&M*)

Left: Vega's scholastic studies at the all-women Barnard College in NYC strongly impacted her songwriting. (*Emily Torem*)

Right: Vega chronicled the landmark St. John Devine Cathedral, a mere sprint from her alma mater, when scribing 'Tom's Diner'. (*Emily Torem*)

Left: When the gridlock of NYC overwhelmed her, Vega sought solace at Riverside Park, with its abundant flora. (*Emily Torem*)

Right: Vega connected universally with her fan base on consistently well-crafted videos.

Left: Flaunting a flair for fashion, the poised chanteuse distills the essence of cinematic Hollywood glamour.

Right: Over the course of her career, Vega added to her wheelhouse by becoming a progenitor of new wave music.

Left: For Vega's fourth Top 20 album in the UK, helmed by Mitchell Froom in 1992, she favored an electronic, experimental oeuvre. (*A&M*)

Right: Vega revamped her sound with producer Froom to create *Nine Objects Of Desire*, a hybrid of industrial soundbites, Latin influences and intense character studies. (*A&M*)

Left: This Rupert Hine-produced 2001 album, which features acoustic guitar, 'dry' vocals and painstaking narratives, ushered back former fans. (*A&M*)

Right: Vega's Blue Note Records debut, with producer Jimmy Hogarth, underscores the grit and garishness of her native New York City. (*Blue Note Records*)

Left: On self-formed label, Amanuensis, with producer Gerry Leonard (Bowie), Vega features her first 'sample' from 50 Cent's 'Candy Shop'. (*Amanuensis Productions, Cooking Vinyl*)

Right: With composer Duncan Sheik, Vega immortalizes Southern writer Carson McCullers's legacy and mystique. (*Amanuensis Productions, Cooking Vinyl*)

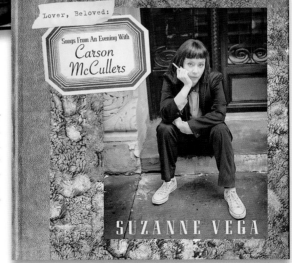

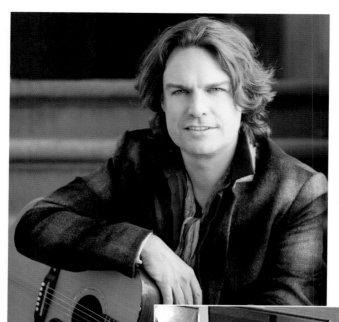

Left: New York-based singer-songwriter Jann Klose, an early support act and fellow traveler, identifies with Vega's passion for 'place'. (*Mikiado*)

Right: Hudson Valley's Jonathan Gordon shows off the teal axe on which he composed the iconic 'Luka' solo. (*Michael Kessler*)

Right: Producer/ songwriter Richard Barone frequently performs with Vega in NYC concert halls. He heavily researched the NYC Greenwich Village scene in *Music and Revolution: Greenwich Village in the 1960s.* (*Michael Stahl*)

Left: Los Angeles-based composer/arranger John Philip Shenale enjoyed Herb Alpert's congeniality at A&M. The label ceased operations in 1999, but Shenale cherished its heyday. (*Marta Woodhull*)

Above: Tony-Award winner, Duncan Sheik, collaborated with Vega for 2016's *Lover Beloved: Songs from an Evening with Carson McCullers.* (*Shervin Lainez*)

Left: Singer-songwriter, Lucy Kaplansky, played a significant role in Vega's early career and is still smitten with Vega's lyrical detail. (*Beowulf Sheehan*)

Above: Studio engineer/guitarist Steve Addabbo recognized Vega's creative potential and successfully co-produced her debut and *Solitude Standing*.

Right: A study in deep blue – Vega's curtain call at the NYC City Winery for the 2017 Marc Bolan 40ᵗʰ Anniversary Celebration. (*Philamonjaro*)

Above: Vega in zebra stripes and signature top hat with Irish producer, guitarist and arranger Gerry Leonard. (*Gerry Leonard*)

Below: Calling all guitarists! Long-term producer, Gerry Leonard, is clearly decked out in royal garb, but what's that shape he's forming? (*Steve Rose*)

Above: Electric and acoustic sonics blend seamlessly when Leonard and Vega perform live. (*Gerry Leonard*)

Right: Despite white, hot lights, Vega remains remarkably cool at S.P.A.C.E in Evanston, Illinois, in 2013. (*Philamonjaro*)

suzanne vega

tom's diner

Left: If a quintessential diner, known colloquially as 'a greasy spoon', could only talk… (*A&M*)

Right: Curious characters inside and beyond the red vinyl booths and plate-glass of Tom's Restaurant inspired 'Tom's Diner'. (*Lisa Torem*)

Above: Tom's Restaurant was Vega's muse, but 'Tom's Diner', in turn, captivated countless cover acts, including DNA, who produced a controversial remix. (*Lisa Torem*)

Right: If I slug down this cuppa Joe, will I write a killer song, too? (*Christopher Torem*)

Left: Dressed in midnight black, the songwriter of 'I Never Wear White' entertains aficionados at S.P.A.C.E. in Evanston, Illinois in 2013. (*Philamonjaro*)

Right: A&M Records, an American label co-founded in 1962 in Santa Monica, California, by Herb Alpert and Jerry Moss, started with a handshake. Alpert was an important figure in Vega's career. (*A&M*)

'I think she was just interested in having her records have a little more projection and a little more intensity.'

Froom also stated that he had been sent a variety of demos from Vega's camp and ultimately decided: 'I liked the acoustic demos better than the band demos she'd done.'

He also intimated that personnel in the past hadn't paid enough attention to Vega's lyrics, and had been more consumed by the prettiness of her voice and her guitar playing. As such, he felt that the music 'should reflect the darkness of what she was talking about.'

Drummer and percussionist Jerry Marotta began playing with Hall and Oates and Peter Gabriel in the late 1970s, as well as with Joan Armatrading and Tears for Fears, among others, in the early to mid-1980s. His compositional ear and cinematic style of drumming added vibrancy to the synthesizer interludes.

The album garnered rave reviews. Journalist Ken Tucker of the *Philadelphia Enquirer* said: 'The sound of the album is a welcome departure for Vega.' Stephen Holden, of *The New York Times*, exclaimed in 1992: '...Vega has taken a large step in defining her artistic identity.'

By all means, Vega's intuition had been spot-on. This bold venture into electronica, wasn't entirely new, of course; she'd made her mark with the remixed 'Tom's Diner', but this was an album dedicated to a new genre, with the instruments playing as much a part as her prose.

And Vega had become, over the years, a more authoritative advocate of her own work. She understood more about the process of establishing collaborative priorities.

In an interview with the author from 2012, Vega explained:

I've learned the most from Mitchell and he was the most challenging, also because there were moments when I didn't always agree with what he said and so I would say, 'That's not appropriate' or 'I don't want to do that,' and that was fine. He set the high watermark. He had a great imagination. He brought everything to the table when he worked, so if I hated something, he would immediately give it up. He wasn't someone who defended his own point of view or inflicted his own methods, but it wasn't always easy. It wasn't always natural, but a lot of it was and I learned so much about music and about production, things that I'm still teaching my daughter today. Mitchell and I worked on that album so quickly and we came up with all of the ideas and the sketches in about two weeks. It was a very quick process and we were both in the same state of mind. I loved everything about that album. It really surpassed my wildest dreams.

'I think we caught a great energy that was happening at that moment in time,' Vega told David Chiu of *Huff Post* on 8 September 2017 when looking back at the album's legacy. She added that: 'Finally, I get to hear songs the way that I feel and hear them in my mind.'

The term '99.9F' works well as a song track title, album title and leitmotif; Vega's soundscapes may vary on this project, but as a collection, the tracks are more incendiary and unpredictable than on previous albums. There's a hot, rebellious streak that Vega and Froom manifested here; it's as though they struck a match over a gasoline can and stubbornly refused to yell 'fire'. Thankfully, these changes were not lost on the popular press. Critics applauded Vega and Froom's work.

Froom became Vega's first husband. Their daughter, Ruby Froom, would eventually contribute vocals to backing tracks on future albums and pursue a career as a singer.

As part of the promotion, Vega agreed to appear on The Howard Stern Interview E show in 1993. In an era, which came well before the 2006 #MeToo movement, a phenomenon that consolidated American women and their allies against harassment, and in which case there might have been a backlash, Vega had to face off a barrage of overt advances, disparaging comments about her choice of clothing and intrusive questions about abuse.

While it was true that this American host was known for bucking the traditional broadcasting system, and that most of his guests knew about his tactics before agreeing to come on the show, his actions were still considered by many viewers to be an overreach, despite the fact that Stern was a positive promoter of Vega's discography.

Vega did her best to deflect Stern's boorish statements and actions – Stern repeatedly asked to kiss her, but her discomfort was visible. Vega did have the opportunity to promote her album during this half-hour debacle, but the promotion came at a cost.

Perhaps Vega's creativity in terms of describing physical objects provides relief from more objectification. That's another reason that her songs about everyday objects strike a chord. In 'Small Blue Thing', an inanimate object 'made of China, made of glass' takes up physical space, but on its own terms.

'Rock in This Pocket (Song of David)' (Suzanne Vega)

That's David Hidalgo, of Los Lobos, playing that go-for-broke electric guitar part, and Richard Pleasance countering Hidalgo with effervescence. Vega's voice flickers in and out of this entertaining tableau, among flashes of clank and boom, where she reframes the ancient biblical story of the meek David and the overwhelmingly strong Goliath. But we know the take-away.

'So small to you, so large to me,' Vega sings, but while those words appear to be innocuous, or simply part of the obligatory scene setting, Vega uses musical twists to elicit empathy for David, the historically persistent underdog.

As she did in 'Small Blue Thing', Vega sees in the ordinary physical object something strong, sacred and lasting that we mere mortals might have missed. She humanizes and contemporizes these familiar characters. Further down the line, she achieves more emotional heights, not only through the familiar storyline but with warm, extended phrases.

'Blood Makes Noise' (Suzanne Vega)

Single releases: UK: 60, US Modern: 1, AUS: 61, NZL: 42

Vega's electronically muffled voice carries an air of authority, as she recites obscure medical terminology, although her utterances often sound like they are emanating from the Holland Tunnel, which I believe was the intent.

Hidalgo retains a steady fist, too, on this excellent techno track. Marvelously in sync with the era, it would have fitted snugly on the Depeche Mode shelf at one's local record shop in the 1980s.

Vega told the BBC's *The Late Show* in 1993 that the song is 'about fear and anxiety in the doctor's office.' She clarifies feelings of being overwhelmed with simple lines about 'ringing in my ear.' Within the framework of the simple images, she illustrates the power structure that exists between doctor and patient, and the resultant patient vulnerability under such circumstances.

Similarly, though, like much of her repertoire, Vega uses poetic devices and persistent clanking in the background, rather than a forceful voice, to get the point across.

B-side: 'Men Will Be Men' (Suzanne Vega) (CD single, Europe only)

Vega wrote this song about touring in the UK – 'they'll call me the guv'nor' and observing the characteristics of her crew. She's in charge, but still amiable and approachable.

Musically, 'Men Will Be Men' is about as close to a lyrical sea shanty as Vega gets. With the buoyant, rhythmic strumming, Vega extends an open invitation to sing along, but thematically it is a forceful song about extending generosity and showing leadership.

It is a simply arranged song (acoustic guitar and voice) and as the verses unfold, we witness the 'guv'nor' acquiring respect and making astute comments that bring the story to life: "Spider' is polite for a second-story man.'

'In Liverpool' (Suzanne Vega)

Single release: UK: 52

Vega revisits her camp counselor crush, whom we met in 'Gypsy', and who actually did come from Liverpool, but other than that, the bold song stands musically in direct opposition to the gentler and more linear 'Gypsy'.

In this innovative story song, Vega assigns the role of bellringer (made famous by the character Quasimodo in *The Hunchback of Notre Dame*) to the erratic and emotionally severed main character.

'Like a hunchback in heaven, he's ringing the bells of the church' – this character rings the bell 'for the last half an hour.' She claims that 'he's crazy' or 'missing something'. We're not exactly clear about his relationship with the female character. Is he pining over their failed relationship? She humbles herself, 'I'll be the girl who sings for my supper,' and then surprises us by ushering in another character: 'You'll be the monk whose forehead is high.' Is this a reference to her belfry buddy or another character altogether?

'In Liverpool' is extremely well-crafted in the instrumental sense. After the second chorus, the electric guitar celebrates the lilting melody.

'99.9F' (Suzanne Vega)
Single release: UK: 46, US Modern: 13
'It could be normal, but it isn't quiet,' Vega sings, with cool observation on the first verse of the album's title-song. Her effervescence is offset by blazing instrumental hits. 'You seem to me to be a man on the verge of burning,' she asserts in the B-section, as we get closer to the core of the context.

Credits on this guitar-driven song go to Blake and Hidalgo for creating an uber-rich tapestry. The '(Shimmy Shimmy) Ko Ko Wop' (El Capris in 1956) rhythm and dreamy layers of indiscrete voices at the chorus offer a respite from the razor-sharp riffs of the verse.

'Could make you want to stay awake at night,' we are warned. Vega's almost robotic repetition, a technique so popular at the time, creates a fascinating, rubber band-about-to-snap tension throughout the arrangement.

'Blood Sings' (Suzanne Vega)
Marc Schulman takes full command of the bouzouki's (a stringed instrument historically used in Greece and Turkey) shimmering, mandolin-type sound. Bassist Michael Visceglia fires on all possible pistons. Vega, revisiting her unplugged days, generates a trembling broken-chord progression and a hypnotic melody.

In reference to meeting her birth father for the first time, Vega alluded to part of the lyrical content to *American Songwriter*, '...it sings to recognize the face.'

'How did this come to pass?' she asks at the chorus, before spiraling into a deeper analysis. She conveys a sense of futile searching, a longing for answers to a befuddling past, and although the process of seeking out one's roots can be daunting, Vega's arrangement doesn't get swept away by sentiment. 'Blood Sings', a brave song, is well-structured and concise.

On *Austin City Limits*, Vega reveals: 'This song is about finding relatives that you never knew you had.' Vega's sensitivity comes through inexplicably with biting insights about abandonment and the desire to connect.

'Fat Man and Dancing Girl' (Suzanne Vega and Mitchell Froom)
Jerry Scheff on double bass and Tchad Blake on electric guitar whip up a whimsical fanfare on this brief, industrial mix. Vega does her bohemian best to explain that her nerves are getting shot when 'monkey in the middle' mucks up her worldview: 'it's making me nervous, get rid of it quick.' The monkey represents a real-life nemesis, a draining, manipulative voice.

The most telling line, though, is 'most of the show is concealed from view.' Vega explained in *The Passionate Eye* that she envisioned 'a shadow puppet' when she conceptualized this song: 'the thing that is really causing the shadow is the thing behind the screen.'

I immediately thought about *The Wizard of Oz,* furiously pushing down levers as Dorothy rushes behind that curtain and looks on in surprise, but Vega's philosophy is less fantastical. She is seemingly tearing down that fake, fourth wall between artist and audience, and perhaps validating her own perspective on performance. With the exception of the occasional black top hat, she has not been known as a flashy performer – a chronic costume changer. 'I don't give a glamorous show,' she admitted to Leonard Cohen. Similarly, to her peer Tracy Chapman, or predecessor Laura Nyro, Vega has ranked poetic lyricism above gimmick or brand.

'(If You Were) in My Movie' (Suzanne Vega)
In a smart set of persuasive verses, Vega imagines her lover serving as a doctor, priest and a gangster, etc., under an aggressive camera lens. With a critical eye for what those occupations entail, and a splash of humor, Vega creates a novelistic, quickly-moving song.

In an interview with Leonard Cohen from *The Passionate Eye*, Vega explains: 'It's a flirting kind of song. It's a song looking at another person and saying these are qualities that you could be, that you could have within you. These are the things that I see.'

Her personification of the song does feel flirtatious; she enjoys the hunt, the variety, the alchemy of acknowledging one's obvious charms, with no strings attached. Everybody wins.

Vega has frequently said in interviews that she enjoys inhabiting other worlds and other characters. As such, she doesn't just dole out an appetizer – we get a rijsttafel.

'As a Child' (Suzanne Vega)
Vega trades off vocals with powerful instrumental riffs when viewing the world through a doll's 'secretive stare' or through the lens of urban inhabitants. Accordingly, 'they seem to have a life.' The personality traits she assigns to the doll, in particular, skim the paranormal, yet the heavily rhythmic background keeps the song grounded in tradition.

Vega uses a persona poem approach in which she speaks directly to the listener in real-time: 'You have a doll. You see this doll,' which brings us immediately into the story's skittish schema.

She builds on the relationship between the doll and the listener in the second verse. When she sings, 'You watch her face,' we become more than observers, we almost become accidental voyeurs, because now, we don't just see the doll's pedestrian, physical form, we see her 'eyes of glass.' She's now somewhat human, although still an enigma.

Then, Vega shifts to a more neutral tone. 'She seems to...,' she repeats, 'have a life.' But in the next verse, she abandons the doll. We're left to 'pick up sticks' on the infectious street.

The emotion comes back in full force as the lyric becomes more intimate. Now, she sings, 'as a child you see yourself.' She describes that new being as someone who is immobilized physically. Emotionally, too, she is at a standstill. Have we become one with the glassy-eyed doll?

In the final verse, she has come full circle. It appears that we've grown up now. It may be difficult, but you 'learn to have a life.'

'Bad Wisdom' (Suzanne Vega)

Over a stark, but escalating Jacques Brel background, Vega brings to light a story of sexual violence and a palpable set of after-effects. A survivor's mother refuses to offer emotional support. In fact, her 'eyes grow cold' and the young woman eventually takes to the streets.

As with 'Luka,' another song chronicling abuse, Vega illustrates trauma through direct, intelligible lyrics, rather than vocal histrionics. As the story grows grimmer, Vega remains the steady, omniscient voice who earns our trust, by meting out evocative detail in a cinematic and believable way.

'When Heroes Go Down' (Suzanne Vega)

Released as a single in 1993. UK: 58, AUS: 113

With zesty, garage rock splendor, Vega exclaims, 'You can't expect any kind of mercy from a battlefield.' 'When heroes go down, they land in flame,' Vega sings in the second verse. She already explained in the first verse: 'they go down fast.'

It's a theme which many pop songwriters and vocalists have eagerly explored, and with a similar degree of emotion over the years, although Vega aims for the jugular.

John Lennon penned 'Working Class Hero' in 1970, David Bowie wrote 'Heroes' in 1977 and Bonnie Tyler sang 'Holding Out For a Hero' in 1984, the focus was on idealism.

In contrast, Vega's version is realistic. There are no allusions; no currying favor for a larger-than-life ideal. This tune has a somber, intriguing twist which brings to mind Bob Dylan's skinny on skepticism revealed on the 1965 'Subterranean Homesick Blues' when he griped: 'Don't follow leaders, watch the parking meters.' Similarly, Vega refuses to get maudlin.

'As Girls Go' (Suzanne Vega)

Vega described the real-life subject, a waitress, as one who was 'utterly charismatic' and 'very graceful' in the *New York Press*, Volume 12, Issue 21. Vega was entranced by the way the woman, who in actuality was a man, moved effortlessly through physical space.

Although intrigued by the emotional effect that this person had on her, she refused to be intrusive, so, with no need for further explanation about the character's motivations, she respectfully recreated a unique moment in time. She conveys the subject's beauty and intrigue and sums up her reaction innocently and non-judgmentally in the repetitive chorus line, which doubles as the title.

Richard Thompson's invigorating guitar work is a major ingredient; the British virtuoso encapsulates the thematic magnetism. The outro solo shines as well. With heed to the hi hat and a throbbing bassline, the instrumental portion reigns.

'Song of Sand' (Suzanne Vega, Nils Petter Molvaer)

This co-write is ushered in and built upon David Hidalgo's tender classical guitar accompaniment, which is a fitting backdrop for Vega's heartfelt story. What follows is a hybrid of tear-stained guitar and searing electronic ambience.

The chordal structure is straightforward, deriving its strength from a constant interplay once more between bright major and sad minor tonalities.

Vega begins this unique anti-war song (the Gulf War) with a breathtaking, but clinical comparison of sand waves versus sound waves. Then, on the second verse, she deviates from the dreamy poetic imagery and adds vulnerable human beings to the fold. There are no quick and dirty answers, of course, but Vega's questions truly provoke: 'What kind of rule can overthrow a fool and leave the land with no stain?'

'Private Goes Public' (Suzanne Vega)

Outside the U.S., 'Private Goes Public' appeared as a bonus track on the UK, European and Japanese version of the CD. It's the unnerving backstory of an introverted entertainer whose social anxiety increases when coping with the discomfort of fame.

The intricate guitar work becomes increasingly more evocative during each stanza. This short, but very focused song could easily fit into a Jacques Brel or Bertolt Brecht retrospective due to its rambling guitar and cutting imagery.

Private Goes Public' is reminiscent of the translucent 'Night Vision' from *Solitude Standing* ('half the world is weakness, the other in fear') and 'Big Space' (*Days of Open Hand*), in which Vega also disentangles feelings of alienation and anonymity.

Nine Objects of Desire (1996)

Personnel
Suzanne Vega: vocals and guitar
Mitchell Froom: keyboards, Moog bass, string and horn arrangements
Tchad Blake: guitar, whistle, effects, mixing
Steve Donnelly: guitar
Dave Douglas: trumpet
Don Byron: clarinet
Jane Scarpantoni: cello
Mark Feldman: strings
Sebastian Steinberg: bass
Bruce Thomas: bass
Yuval Gabay: drums
Jerry Marotta: drums, percussion
Pete Thomas: drums, drum loop, percussion
Produced by Mitchell Froom at The Magic Shop, New York, 10 September 1996
Label: A&M
Release date: 10 September 1996
Highest chart places: UK (OCC): 43, US Billboard 100: 92
Running time: 38:52
Album Art: On one of her most attractive covers, Vega centers a green apple in front of her right eye. You'll have to listen to the album to discover the identity of the eight other objects.

S. Mirkin at *ew.com* on 20 September 1996 referred to the dozen tracks of Vega's fifth studio album, *Nine Objects of Desire,* as 'a stunning collection that's simultaneously sensuous and thought provoking' and comparable to The Beatles' *Revolver.*

Froom, at the helm again as producer, co-writes two tracks. Hidalgo has left the building. Jerry Marotta is as paramount in the arena of percussion, as he'd been in *99.9F.*

Drummer Pete Thomas, bassist Bruce Thomas and guitarist Stephen Donnelly are actively involved, with Froom asserting synth effects, but to a lesser degree than on *99.9F.*

Vega's themes include marriage and childbirth; she veers away from some of the politically conscious storylines that evolved on the last album. She passionately embraces her early Latin musical influences – in fact, one can imagine her putting Astrid Gilberto's rendition of 'Girl from Ipanema' on repeat before heading into the studio.

Although the focus of this book is on studio work, it's important to acknowledge Vega's role outside the studio as an influencer and supporter of other female artists. During the *Days of Open Hand* time period, women-identifying artists began to seek more commercial validation in outdoor festivals, such as Sarah McLachlan's female-focused Lilith Fair tours, which would undergo an initial three-year iteration and resurface years later.

This was a phenomenon for which Vega enthusiastically took part. As such, she came onboard for this one-off spectacle in its first year, which took place in 1997. At that time, Canadian organizer and singer-songwriter Sarah McLachlan, was the featured act. McLachlan formed the festival after enduring years of frustration as a female performer.

She told *Vanity Fair* on 30 September 2019 in the article, 'Building a Mystery: An Oral History of Lilith Fair' by J. Hopper, and with S. Geffen and Jenn Pelly, that she continued to hear from promoters: 'No, we can't play your song – we already have another woman artist in rotation. No, you can't put two women on the same concert bill – it's box office poison.' Lilith Fair offered women an opportunity to collaborate with other female acts and promote their material freely.

During the second year, which took place from 19 June until 31 August 1998, Vega was a major headliner, along with Sinead O'Connor, Lauryn Hill, Queen Latifah and Bonnie Raitt, and others.

In the third year, which took place from 8 July to 31 August 1999, Vega also headlined and performed with, among others, Meshell Ndegeocello and The Pretenders. Eventually, her featured role in the festival diminished, but Vega continued to rally behind the cause of a festival that proclaimed women as viable, commercial entities, at a time when radio and concert promoters were still reluctant to book more than one female act on a show or bill.

The UK outlet *Music Week* gave the album a five-star rating on 15 February 1997, with *Rolling Stone* coming in at four.

'Birth-day' (Love Made Real)' (Suzanne Vega)

Vega's visceral opening song is about childbirth and the promise of the future. Within that framework, she displays an extraordinary vocal range and intensity. The initial breathy phrases are surrounded by a cacophony of sonics. Manic drum fills follow. The loopy melody cascades through complex harmonic changes.

In the B-section, when Vega splays us on the gurney, it's not a rosy ride: 'Strap me down from wrist to heel'. The juxtaposition between physical pain and the miracle of birth makes this a unique song, not to mention that the Hammond organ also makes a surprise appearance.

'Headshots' (Suzanne Vega, Mitchell Froom)

Ushered in by Pete Thomas's military drumming and Tchad Blake's sample of a human whistle, this co-write by Vega and Froom is a loosely articulated portrait of a young man: 'two eyes in the shade, a mouth so sad and small ...'

The story revolves around this indistinct character, who could be anybody hoping to achieve stardom, but in the third verse, the story turns personal: 'the days we were together and I knew that you loved me.'

'Caramel' (Suzanne Vega)

Although 'Caramel' was used in the trailer for *Closer* and on the soundtrack of *The Truth About Cats and Dogs*, this film noir Bossa Nova classic would be well-suited for a myriad of other films. 'Caramel' is memorable because it features one of Vega's most subtle but compelling vocal performances where she mimics a mysterious vixen who longs for lasting love but can't seem to achieve her goal.

Dave Douglas's muted trumpets and Cecelia Sparacio's ethereal flute convey much of the 1960s Latin vibe that inspired Vega in her youth, particularly the Antonio Carlos Jobim composed 1965 classic, 'Girl From Ipanema', made famous by velvet-voiced Astrud Gilberto.

The Smithereens, a 1980s, New Jersey band, originally comprised of guitarist Jim Babjak, drummer Dennis Diken and bassist Mike Mesaros, and fronted by the late, multi-talented singer-songwriter Patrick DiNizio, were also fans of Gilberto. (They now continue as a trio).

The group caught on to Vega's similarly cool sound and asked her to sing harmonies and a few lines in the verses to DiNizio's original song, 'In a Lonely Place' for their 1986 debut album, *Especially For You*.

Charles Wittenmeier's video features classic movie scenes and keenly captures the cinematic quality of the subject's bliss and ultimate disillusionment. Vega is shown in a variety of glamorous vintage evening gowns under soft lights in full femme fatale fashion.

This beautiful ballad evokes a time when romantic subtlety in music and film trumped ostentatious language and behavior.

'Stockings' (Suzanne Vega, Mitchell Froom)

'Passion' or 'friendship'? What path does a physical attraction take? In the early verses, Vega's story revolves around a female prototype who stirs up a number of relational possibilities that may lie 'between the binding of her stocking and her skin.'

In an album where every song revolves around a unique setting, 'Stockings' can't really get its due, but it's a delightful, cleverly worded confection with a 1960s beat and a devilish bassline. The snappy lyric predates what follows with Vega's Carson McCullers-centered work.

'Casual Match' (Suzanne Vega, Mitchell Froom)

Unlike 'Stockings,' 'Casual Match' is heavily produced, with predictable jackhammer percussive sounds that come across like slick slaps against an unstable wooden desk. The dissonant harmonies on the cheerful chorus are lively and fun. The husky, prominent bassline frames the song perfectly.

While the message in 'Stockings' is completely clear, I'm feeling less of a connection here. While the lyrics are beautifully stated, especially in the repeated chorus – 'fire and ash is the season's yield' – I find myself asking: is this a metaphor about a human relationship relative to nature?

'Thin Man' (Suzanne Vega)

This is a haunting song about the grim reaper with a thrilling, funky beat. On the surface, however, the arrangement passes muster as an enthralling and sensual love song. 'I can feel his eyes when I don't expect him,' Vega sings, and if a shrug could be depicted sonically, it would sound this way.

The angular melody lends itself to a host of textures, to which rising horns and trickles of electric guitar oblige. The Wurlitzer piano doesn't fall far behind.

What's best is how Vega's voice retains a confident couth against the pronounced riffery, but I also thoroughly enjoyed the energetic instrumental interlude.

'No Cheap Thrill' (Suzanne Vega)

Single releases: UK: 40, US AAA: 12

'No Cheap Thrill' is set in a gambling casino, where the narrator refuses to be short-changed. Vega's snippy card-shark-talk peppers the phrases, but you're duly warned: 'It will cost you, but it's no cheap thrill.'

Vega displays her wit and 'five-card stud' vernacular while namechecking shady fictional characters, the likes of 'Lame brain Pete' and 'Butcher Boy.' This arrangement is a joy, not only because of the striking vocals and sheer backing harmonies, but because the word salad syncs up so well with the cool back beats.

'World Before Columbus' (Suzanne Vega)

Vega describes a world of pre-Columbian riches and wealth that doesn't in the least compare to the satisfaction she receives from being mother to her daughter Ruby. 'World Before Columbus' has a deceptive title, but the message is clear, it's a song about unconditional love. This is a well-crafted, richly arranged love song. Moreover, Vega discovered a unique way in which to describe the fragile bond between parent and child.

'Lolita' (Suzanne Vega, Mitchell Froom)

'Don't beg for some little crumb of affection,' the singer urges. Here, Vega assumes the role of a concerned, experienced woman who elects to warn a young innocent about the wild, unpredictable world beyond, especially in terms of fielding unwanted advances: 'Hey girl,' she hisses, 'I've been where you are standing.'

Harmonies erupt from some other world, rising up like an inquisitive siren. The arrangement leans toward a 'Oye Como Va' vibe with accented Afro-Cuban drumming and liquid instrumental accents. You'll enjoy the slow, steamy build!

'Honeymoon Suite' (Suzanne Vega)

With a return to the strophic form and powerful, linear lyrics, Vega recounts a momentous evening and morning in France with her 'husband,' where spirits lie creepily in wait. This is an exploratory song with many a twist.

The sing-song acoustic guitar is at the forefront, but a series of bleeps seep in that are reminiscent of The Beatles' 'Revolution 9.'

It's a honeymoon wrought with confusion; Vega reaches out to the concierge at the hotel and gets rebuffed whilst her 'husband,' after a night of feeling ill, wonders what went on in the room, yet Vega's voice remains calm and somewhat stoic as she retells the ghost-like story.

'Tombstone' (Suzanne Vega)
At a live performance, Vega said that this old-timey, piano-driven romp (on the original recording) was actually inspired by a familial Viking cat funeral, but in practice, 'Tombstone' is a spirited and charming song.

'I like a tombstone 'cause it weathers well,' Vega sings glibly on the first verse. 'If you carve my name in marble you must cut it deep,' she declares in the second verse. The tag line about 'burning' refers to the actual ritualistic act of cremation. The humor, however, stems from Vega's deadpan approach to dealing with the grim reaper. She displays great wit with these concrete, easy-listening lyrics.

She rearranged the song with finger snaps on *Close-Up, Volume 3*, with Gerry Leonard playing full-on guitar with glistening effects. Fans are divided on which arrangement they prefer instrumentally: the original piano version or the later guitar version. Leonard more than keeps up the pace, yet that clanking, old-timey piano is hard to resist.

'My Favorite Plum' (Suzanne Vega)
While Vega has become known for her creative metaphors, this one takes her writing to new heights, with its sly innuendo: 'My favorite plum hangs so far from me' and 'See how the flesh presses the skin.'

The compelling bass line on the baritone guitar closely follows Vega's contralto in the verse, creating a Sergio Leone feel. The symphonic sounds of the B-section lie in contrast. This is a romantic song, sung serenely, with logical instrumental transitions between the image-rich phrases. Moreover, the subtle strains of the Hammond B3 contribute to the sensual vibe.

Songs in Red and Gray (2001)

Personnel:
Suzanne Vega: vocals and acoustic guitar
Gerry Leonard: electric and acoustic guitars, dulcimer, mandolin, zither
Rupert Hine: keyboards, bass guitar, percussion, drum programming,
Mike Visceglia: bass guitar
Nik Pugh: drum programming, synth lead
Jay Bellerose: drums
Matt Johnson: drums
Doug Yowell: drums, percussion
Pamela Sue Mann: backing vocals, harmony vocals
Elizabeth Taubman: harmony vocals
Stephen W. Tayler: recording and mixing engineer
Produced by Rupert Hine at Chun King, Sear Sound, Shelter Island Sound,
Looking Glass Studio (New York) on 25 September 2001
Label: A&M
Release date: 25 September 2001
Highest chart places: UK (OCC): 100, US Billboard 200: 178
Running time: 45:31
Album Art: Against a muted wash of autumnal colors, with long, dark hair
flailing against bare shoulders, Vega exhibits the quintessential 'female gaze'
courtesy of Melanie Nissen's lens.

There was a significant gap between the release of *Nine Objects of Desire* and
Songs in Red and Gray. Froom and Vega's divorce, and the aftermath of that
dissolution markedly crept its way into several of the thirteen tracks.

Outside the studio, times were especially volatile. The release date was
merely two weeks after an unexpected tragedy took place. The United
States was still reeling in the wake of the early morning terrorist attack of
11 September 2001 – thereafter referred to as 9/11 – when hijacked planes
crashed into the Twin Towers of The World Trade Center, New York City,
killing employees, passengers and first responders.

'The city that never sleeps,' was at a standstill. While eventually, things
that certain citizens had always taken for granted like efficient plane travel,
community resources, health care and normal school hours resumed, grieving
and a sense of uncertainty continued for months. New Yorkers sought
comfort with friends, family and neighbors, but sorrow lingered in the same
air as the toxic billows of grey smoke that permeated Ground Zero. Although
it was too late to include a song honoring the fallen on this album, Vega
would include the evocative memorial 'Anniversary' on her next studio visit.

Statistics that documented the number of people still missing or dead, plus
the number of remains recovered graced *The New York Times* headlines on
the release date. It would have been easy to disregard the debut, but the city
needed its faithful artists more than ever before.

Despite the emotionally charged factors that predated the record, Vega carried on: With Froom's professional exodus and British producer Rupert Hine soliciting new ideas from his client, Vega had returned to the role of consummate singer-songwriter, sans the blips and bleeps, she'd likely come to expect under Mitchell Froom's auspices.

Hine's impressive CV boasted his work as a James Bond film scorer for *Goldeneye*. He had enjoyed collaborations with Bob Geldof, Peter Gabriel, Chrissie Hyde, Sting, Tina Turner and even the Leningrad Philharmonic Orchestra. Like Vega, Hines (who sadly died in June 2020) took his craft seriously but didn't equate success with fame. He made wise choices, especially when he hired Gerry Leonard as a hard-working, fearless lead guitarist, as Leonard would figure prominently over the years to come as one of Vega's most formidable allies. He had already been familiar with *Solitude Standing* and was already a Vega fan when he joined the team. Sadly, however, Hines died in June of 2020: 'I never wanted to be a rock star, but I've always loved the idea of painting pictures with sound,' the Irish musician told *Songfacts.com* in 2011.

Prior to working with Vega, Gerry Leonard's production hits included Tina Turner's *Private Dancer* in 1984 and Stevie Nicks' *The Other Side of the Mirror* in 1989. He'd worked with Duncan Sheik, another integral ally in Vega's trajectory. Leonard played on David Bowie's album, *Toy*, in early 2000 and subsequently toured with Bowie as musical director. He contributed to *Heathen*, *Reality* and *The Next Day*. He also worked in conjunction with Avril Lavigne, Rufus Wainwright and Laurie Anderson, accumulating a wealth of experience as an arranger, producer and musician.

The all-around instrumentalist had originally been asked to play only a couple of songs for Vega's project, but after an accident which caused her to have mobility issues with her arm, she required more consistent help with guitar-based arrangements and Leonard saved the day. His musical responsibilities increased, and he ultimately contributed exponentially to this project as a multi-instrumentalist. He started gigging with Vega, along with bassist Visceglia.

Leonard maintained a big role in Vega's career both onstage and in the studio thereafter. While the guitarist/producer admired Vega for many of her traits, there was one area in which he was particularly in awe: 'What's interesting about Suzanne as an artist is she's a writer, she's a words person and obviously beautiful as a singer of melody,' Leonard exclaimed on YouTube.

Leonard hails from Dublin, Ireland. By all accounts, he cherished the camaraderie he enjoyed with family and close friends, but he reached a point where his opportunity for professional growth would remain limited if he remained local.

When he studied piano as a youngster with a strict teacher, he got turned off to that instrument, yet everything about the guitar – the look, the feel, the sound – felt right. He talked about his first-choice instrument to *bluebirdreviews.com*: 'I think that the guitar is a great instrument to use as the base for soundscapes because it has got a lot of personality and a lot of overtone to it.'

Leonard didn't come from a musical family, per se, but received support from his jack-of-all trades father, who designed and constructed a guitar out of wood scraps and miscellaneous odds and ends. Eventually, he got his first commercial guitar: a Gibson SG with pickups.

After signing to Island Records in the late 1980s, he was sent to music seminars in New York City. After a few trips, he fell in love with the energy and openness 'the big apple' offered.

When Leonard relocated there in the mid-1990s, without a definitive plan, he soon found himself low on financial resources, but he made a name for himself as a session musician through word-of-mouth, and worked in bands like Spooky Ghost (his studio pseudonym). As word got out that he could create ambient, as well as rough-hewn rock sounds, he became a hot commodity. Before long, he found himself in demand by A-list artists.

He ace-d an audition for Cyndi Lauper and toured with the singer and her band in Japan, and then, when serving as musical director for David Bowie on the 2003/2004 *Reality* Tour, he had an epiphany – similarly, to how Vega constructs a story-song, with a definitive beginning, middle and end, Leonard learned to create and commit to musical passages, without second-guessing himself. This new awareness increased his self-confidence in the studio and onstage.

Having lived through a multitude of eras, where guitarists clamored to do solos, as in classic rock, or resisted doing them, because of punk sensibilities, Leonard added a strong degree of self-restraint and a greater awareness of art versus grandstanding to his technical toolbox. Moreover, he was receiving acclaim for developing a unique style. He told Giovanni 'Gio' Pilato of *bluebirdreviews.com* on 24 March 2019:

So, you know, in a strange way, I think that the style that I have ended up with, it is this combination of elements, which is not your straightforward rock 'n' roll guitar or a more traditional style of playing but something that has kind of developed naturally.

Leonard ultimately made a name for himself as a live instrumentalist who creates infectious loops and layers instantaneously, without benefit of pre-recorded music. He brought the same sense of spontaneity to the studio setting when working with Vega, as he did with Bowie.

He also makes liberal use of a series of carefully selected pedals, with the objective being to create distinctive tonal colors. When it comes to melody, he enjoys experimenting with modes, but the bottom line is that when he works with Vega in the studio, he follows his intuition, concentrating fully on the track at hand.

Leonard continued to wear many hats as Vega's colleague. He'd gain a reputation as a fine instrumentalist, but he'd also become known as a go-to co-arranger. To that end, he explained to *CB6 Show: Indie Pop* on 29 September 2021 how the process often worked:

We did flesh out the songs a lot. I remember being in the room making the record and being like, 'What if we did this? We need a riff here. Yeah, okay, let's do that.' I was always firing off, like what we do in a band. 'This bridge is messed up. Why can't we get out of here better?' So, we'd change it to make it better. In the absence of anything else, I probably ended up playing guitar more than I should have, that was without being asked at the time.

The album marked a return to Greenwich Village Vega. She was writing again, without the benefit of a collaborator, and emphasizing lyrical content. She seemed happy at home in her return to the folk idiom, even including a co-write by Jack Hardy. She had come full circle.

After the album's completion, and prior to embarking on another studio project, Vega had another exciting, but unexpected opportunity come her way. While moonlighting as a landscaper, photographer and documentary maker, Christopher Seufert came upon Vega's home in Cape Cod and left a note asking her to consider being a subject for a film project. She got back to Seufert, but not with a related response; it was instead with a request to do a shoot in Manhattan with merely a couple of weeks lead time. Despite having little time to spare to set up, Seufert met the challenge – Vega greenlit the project.

Moving forward, he had the opportunity to watch Vega attend a Greenwich Village songwriter's meeting and perform live in the UK and Europe. When discussing the criteria for what would be considered appropriate shots, the filmmaker and artist reached a quid pro quo. Vega's everyday activities, often centering around rehearsals or live performance, would dominate the final cuts.

'I don't mind being filmed for a documentary, since it allows the camera to see me when I'm in action, and then I don't have to worry about posing. I hate posing! This approach shows me at my best,' she told Randy Steinberg, for the article, 'Man in The Mooncusser,' on 1 September 2003, at *newenglandfilm.com*. Currently, the film is still in progress, but excerpts can be seen on YouTube.

Regarding the album reviews, on 28 September 2001, *Entertainment* wrote: 'Infinite sadness, hypnotic beauty.' In early October, *Mojo*: 'Could well be her finest yet.'

'Penitent' (Suzanne Vega)
Vega explores and struggles with spirituality through tidy turns-of-phrase and biblical riffs. It's not clear to whom she's addressing her pointed questions: a deity, former friend or lover, but she pores her poetic and vocal soul into the quest.

This deep dive was inspired by a visit to a church in the Tuscany region. Awe-struck by the setting, she penned open-hearted lyrics such as: 'forgive me all my blindness's …'

The nature-driven lines to this opener are stark and beautiful: 'I look for you in heathered moor, the desert and the ocean floor.' At the core, the truculent guitar arrangement and sweeping melodic line mirror Dolly Parton's tear-stained ballad, 'Jolene'.

Although the title word never appears, the story is self-explanatory. We don't discover how far she has come in this sacred pilgrimage, but it's easy to assume through her earnest delivery that she has reflected deeply and that her desire to find clarity is sincere.

'Widow's Walk' (Suzanne Vega)
US AAA: 6
'It's not the man, but it's the marriage that was drowned,' Vega intones with conviction. A sense of shock and understandable loss post-divorce is evidenced more through lyrical content than vocal phrasing in the verse.

It's in the chorus that she elicits goosebumps, with intrepid, rising vocals at the cadence points. She draws nautical parallels, uses stunningly bold idioms, and codifies that grief with a clear-headed sense of sequence: 'I knew that ship was empty by the time it hit the rocks.'

But this is not a song sung by a blindsided victim: rather than resorting to 'sour grapes,' Vega reflects back with introspection, painting herself as a knowledge-seeker: 'It's clear that I need better skill in steering.'

'(I'll Never Be) Your Maggie May' (Suzanne Vega)
'Maggie May,' a popular Liverpool sea shanty regarding a street walker and sailor, goes back more than a hundred years. The subject inspired British singer Rod Stewart and garnered the British entertainer a hit in 1971. But even if Vega's female subject was inspired by the ancient nautical tune, the similarities, I believe, end there.

In Vega's guitar-drenched, strongly-feminist folk epic, which brings to mind predecessors such as Lesley Gore with 'You Don't Own Me' or Gloria Gaynor's 'I Will Survive,' Vega crossed the Rubicon, scratching a deep line across the sand. Her courtship will be contingent upon mutually agreed-upon conditions, and certainly without objectification. In a similar vein, Dar Williams continued the consciousness-raising with 'I Won't Be Your Yoko Ono.'

'It Makes Me Wonder' (Suzanne Vega)
After a blister of sonic effects in the introduction, Vega goes full-on strength: 'Who could live up to this?' she inquires. In yet another exploratory theme (which appears to be the hallmark of this thought-provoking album), she name-checks the Virgin Mary amid a cascade of harmonies, and rifles through

a quizzical love affair. The thread of inquiry continues throughout this essentially spiritual quest.

Interestingly, the quickly moving, complex chord progression has a personality all its own, which adds to the mesmerizing quality of this unique song.

'Soap and Water' (Suzanne Vega)

Vega ruminates about Froom and daughter Ruby. In an act of self-actualization or even quiet defiance, she slips off her wedding band but concurrently celebrates her 'little kite.' Producer Hine's synth modestly echoes the haunting melody.

'Soap and Water' relies on a more standard chordal progression, fearless acoustic guitar and waves of strings. Sequentially, this was a good move.

Vega uses both diminutives and acerbic descriptors when depicting the roles of 'mommy' and 'daddy,' but when depicting her daughter, her qualifiers are pure and unambiguous.

'Songs in Red and Gray' (Suzanne Vega)

Accented by passionate classical guitar, Vega rehashes her post-divorce confusion and seemingly struggles with whom to blame. Predictably, Vega remains sympathetic to the child, sandwiched uncomfortably in the middle of the conflict.

The chord progression is fairly standard, allowing for the words to take center stage. The transitional instrumental break is highlighted by delicate broken piano chords and Vega's sheer, soft harmonies. Her craft as a storyteller shines as she takes on a difficult subject without succumbing to cliché or repetition.

'Last Year's Troubles' (Suzanne Vega)

Vega dishes over 'the waifs of Dickensian England,' staid petticoats, robbers and pirates in the perceived days of yore, where fashion and innocence reigned, as opposed to current times, where she cites violence and a growing sense of ennui. Ironically, the World Trade Tower collapsed just a week or so after the album was released.

Both the melody and chorus are bouncy and catchy, and pleasantly anchored with breezy, call-and-response harmonies.

Vega wisely used the efficient strophic style to overlay her quick-witted, tongue-in-cheek observations. Leonard's intricate guitar licks peer out of random corners and contribute exuberantly to the gaiety.

'Priscilla' (Suzanne Vega)

This strophic dirge is backed by intricate instrumentals. Vega illuminates and idealizes a curious friendship with an older ballet dancer, whose shoes are designed from ribbon and whose skirt boasts 'layers of chiffon.'

But similar to most of Vega's repertoire, there's a more complex meaning hidden beneath the obvious commentary: 'We were in costume, this was a game.' Vega characterizes the 20-year age difference between the characters as merely 'awkward,' yet her emphasis on the gap suggests a judgment.

'If I Were a Weapon' (Suzanne Vega)

This marvelously upbeat maverick moves along at an amiable clip. Through her classic style of song-whispering, she takes on a palpable topic: human destruction.

Because Vega has a subdued tone to her voice, the references to dangerous street weaponry are especially frightening. Her measured tone brings to mind the classroom teacher who lowers her voice, when angry, rather than screaming, yet brings the students to tears.

The other twinge of discomfort comes from the matter-of-fact assignment of roles. She tells the other character that he/she would be 'a hammer': 'blunt and heavy at the end and coming down on me.' From title to execution, this is a powerful piece.

'Harbor Song' (Suzanne Vega)

In this song about desperation, longing and disappointment, Vega surmises: 'Your fickle heart will never be true.' She takes ample time to narrate and reflect, using simple images of salty air and, of course, a distant harbor as a haunting leitmotif and metaphorical device.

In contrast to the other songs on the album, 'Harbor Song' has a decidedly jazzy patina, evidenced mostly by the slightly rubato melody and seconded by Astrud Gilberto-esque vocals.

The production is steamy and seamless, featuring a flawless bassline and crisp percussion. 'Harbor Song' signifies one of Vega's most endearing, well-enunciated vocal performances.

'Machine Ballerina' (Suzanne Vega)

The instrumental portion features Ollie W. Tayler's rich, carnivalesque imagination. The curious organ sound is highly original and whimsical.

Thematically, Vega questions her relationship with a judgmental partner. She wonders: how is she being perceived? Is she disposable? Replaceable?

With a flurry of clever qualifiers, interspersed with solid instrumental hooks, Vega configures a world rife with inequity, which she actively attempts to challenge and even deconstruct.

The rapid-fire lyrics are balanced out with spirited instrumental interludes and a brief, transcendental B-section, featuring a chromatic run.

'Solitaire' (Suzanne Vega)

I'm hearing a lyrical nod to Lou Reed in Vega's slick vocals. This uncluttered arrangement finds Nick Pugh doubling on percussion and synth, while Vega excels on plaintive acoustic guitar. On *Close-Up Vol. 3*, the infectious guitar riff moves center stage.

Vega's voice is loose, cunning and country-casual. Production-wise, one can hear clearly her crisp diction; it sounds as though she's merely stepping away despite the sense that, according to the title, she's accustomed to being a shut-in.

'St. Clare' (Jack Hardy) (Suzanne Vega)

For the sole cover on this studio album, Vega spares no emotion. Inspired by the original songwriter and mentor, Jack Hardy, this ballad is poetic, with a focus on the frailty of nature and romantic love. The arrangement is primarily folk guitar-driven but enhanced by sweeping strings.

Hardy's influence on Vega, both instrumentally and thematically, cannot be overstated. Vega's clear-voiced, beautifully articulated rendition of this song puts both songwriters inside the room, technically and emotionally. It's a divine melody and the content is packed with passion.

'Golden' (Japanese CD release only) (Suzanne Vega)

This delightfully pop-influenced love song complete with male backup vocals went missing outside of Japan. Our loss; their gain.

Beauty & Crime (2007)

Personnel:
Suzanne Vega: acoustic guitar and vocals
Gerry Leonard: electric guitar (1, 2, 5-11), acoustic guitar (4, 5, 10)
Lee Renaldo: electric guitar (1, 2, 10)
Martin Slattery: piano (3, 4, 7, 10), flute (9), brass (3), reeds (3)
Samuel Dixon: bass (2, 3, 6, 11), live bass (8)
Tony Shanahan: bass (1, 5, 9, 10)
Mike Visceglia: bass (4)
Graham Hawthorne: drums (1, 3, 5, 6, 9 to 11), live drums (2, 7, 8)
Jimmy Hogarth: percussion (1-5, 10, 11), electric guitar (1), acoustic guitar (11)
Doug Yowell: drums (4, 6), percussion (4, 6)
KT Tunstall: background vocals, arrangements (1, 5)
Ruby Froom: background vocals: (2, 8)
Beccy Byrne: background vocals (8)
Emily Singer: background vocals (8)
Anthony Genn: background vocals (11)
Philip Sheppard: cello (1, 6, 7)
Matthew Ward: violin (1, 7)
London Studio Orchestra: strings (2, 4, 7, 9) led by Perry Montague-Mason
Pete Davis: programming (2, 4, 7, 8, 10)
Label: Blue Note, Capitol
Produced by Jimmy Hogarth at Great City Productions and Sear Sound Studios, New York City, Jimmy's Studio and Olympic Studios, London, England, 17 July 2007.
Cameron Craig: engineer
Emery Dobyns: engineer
Tchad Blake: mixing engineer
Bob Ludwig: mastering engineer
Release date: 17 July 2007
Highest chart places: UK Albums: 127, US Billboard 200: 129
Running time: 33:58
Album Art: Dressed in classic black, with an oversized beret tipped over an eye, Vega exemplifies the Hollywood glam that she opts to celebrate through stylized songs.

During the six-year period that took place between the release of *Songs in Red and Gray* and the development of *Beauty & Crime*, Vega had her hands full. Besides writing for *The New York Times*, she had made the choice to change management and sign up with the legendary Blue Note Records, a historically jazz-oriented label that gained continued credibility from bebop's holy trinity: Thelonious Monk, Charlie Parker and Dizzy Gillespie, and down the road Wayne Shorter, John Coltrane and Miles Davis, among others.

Vega set out to find another open-minded producer. By this point, she'd seen herself through the neo-folk and industrial lens; she'd co-written and arranged, and of course, written solely by herself, but there were other spheres to conquer.

As such, she developed a creative relationship with British producer Jimmy Hogarth, whose roster included the late Amy Winehouse, Sia, Duffy and Tina Turner. Hogarth and Vega developed studio chemistry at the get-go and the industry would take note. Along with Tchad Blake, Cameron Craig and Emery Dobyns, the Scottish producer would win a Grammy for Best Engineered Album, Non-Classical for *Beauty & Crime*.

US Singles Top 100 Hits included 'Umbrella' by Rihanna and Jay-Z, 'Big Girls Don't Cry' by Fergie, 'Makes Me Wonder' by Maroon 5, 'Summer Love' by Justin Timberlake and 'Rehab' by Amy Winehouse.

Vega may have felt fine about being considered alternative, but how would she fare with the current youth market? She'd been away from the studio for a considerable length of time. How challenging would it be to reinvent herself once again? Would she appeal to the same fan base? Could she make headway with new fans?

Fortunately, there were multiple variables in her favor. She had an opportunity to shake the trees with this new album because she had at her disposal a fresh palette of colors and textures. The album wouldn't simply be a rose-colored love story, per se, about New York City, it would play out with a raw, unconditional perspective. With *Beauty & Crime*, Vega mirrored and mapped out the temptations, as well as the darkest cul-de-sacs of her hometown.

Some tracks dignify her favorite haunts; she empowers them as hotbeds of culture, but at other turns, she renders her city a bastion of decay. Vega's shifting perspectives are poignant. Sometimes, she sees New York City through the lens of an innocent muse. But at other times, she's like a construction worker on a scaffold with a bird's eye view; an omniscient observer, fully conscious of the chaos and congestion, but with the capacity to rise above it and see human behavior as flawed, but functional.

It's clear that Vega went to great lengths to complete this project. And putting theme aside, there were sounds she was anxious to excavate. Vega explained on a promotional YouTube video:

I wanted to combine cool rhythms and cool beats. Everybody's always doing these albums of standards and classics so I loved those orchestrations and I wanted to see what my voice would sound like against the strings and the horns.

As such, Vega elected to write new, original songs but 'with that old-style orchestration.' But is it not true that 'no good deed goes unpunished?'

On 25 March 2022, for 'Closeup with Suzanne Vega,' Vega told Paul Sinclair at *superdeluxe.com* that she loved 'Blue Note' and 'I had a great time there. But I had an album [with them] that came out and won a Grammy and then I was dropped!' She added, 'which was a shock.'

Vega had only been involved with Blue Note for two years. She had no choice but to quickly reestablish her career. Because the label still retained her master recordings, she set in motion a pattern that other artists would logically follow: Vega re-arranged her original music, for which she still owned the rights.

This led to a wellspring of alternative studio projects and a crash course in social media promotion. Between Facebook and Twitter, Vega would galvanize fans and encourage their feedback, but finally, on her own terms.

With Evan Toth in September 2021, she discussed reactions to the *Beauty & Crime* reissue: 'We recorded it on analogue and then digitalized it. We had the best of both worlds. We had the warmth of the analogue world and we had the ease of the digital world.'

'Zephyr & I' (Suzanne Vega)

Graham Hawthorne created a mellow mood with a rigorous backbeat in the introductory measures of this urban story-song about a West End friendship between Vega and acclaimed graffiti artist, Zephyr. The contagious, repetitive instrumental hook is reminiscent of Lou Reed's 'Vicious', although the similarities abruptly end there.

Vega switches casually from head to chest voice within measures and KT Turnstall's lithe harmonies are a joy to behold. Gerry Leonard and Lee Renaldo handle strident guitar riffs.

At the chorus, the buddies reminisce about the 1970s: 'the kids are gone, but the souls remain.' Vega's voice stays warm and focused as she envisions a cleansing rain, the life cycle of flowers and eradicated graffiti.

However, at the B-section, the instrumentals dissolve into off-beat psychedelia, with Philip Sheppard's cutting cello at the helm.

'Zephyr & I' is a delightful pop confection as an opener, and in that, it's not so profound that we can't comfortably move on to the following track, but it's a stand-up song. It's the linen tablecloth and polished stemware that beckon you to feast. But wait – the big meal will follow.

It's not until the final verse that Vega inserts the word 'fatherless' to describe these faceless teenagers. We were getting to know the gang in a generic sense, but that well-placed qualifier left me wanting to know more about these nameless youths.

'Ludlow Street' (Suzanne Vega)

With the first appearance of the London Studio Orchestra's strings, Vega commemorates her late brother, Tim, who was a graffiti artist. The siblings hung out and frequently reconnected on Ludlow Street. Sadly, Tim died in 2002.

With bright, acoustic guitar against Samuel Dixon's penetrating bass, Hawthorne's 'live' drum kit and Ruby Froom's clear vocals, Vega creates a touching homage. Gerry Leonard's cello line was striking.

The lyrics are heartbreakingly direct; there is no dark curtain to hide behind, no attempt at ambiguity: 'Love is the only thing that matters,' Vega sings, with a slight tear in the throat, but she also goes on to describe this phenomenon as being '...the hardest thing to feel.'

Those who have faced grief may feel a similarly large lump in the throat. The nuances include Leonard's subtle, poignant cello line. The theme, in and of itself, is evergreen.

'New York is a Woman' (Suzanne Vega)
Vega uses metaphor brilliantly when describing her city's curious parallels to a human female. Both entities reveal a rugged constitution juxtaposed with a quiet beauty. More to the point, there are 'bangles and spangles,' but also 'scars.' At the chorus, when Vega admits: 'she's every dame you've ever seen on late night TV,' the grease paint wins over the glamor.

The song is a tease; a dance, a peek into post-war American musical slang. Vega seems to view New York as a siren that remains out of mortal reach. You may admire her fair city from a distance or hate her in plain sight, but you won't get close enough to possess her; it's an unrequited affair.

Martin Slattery's piano arrangement guarantees a fitting Broadway glam. There's no excess musical activity here, with mainly Hamilton on drums and Hogarth on percussion – Vega's savvy prose monopolizes the masthead.

'Pornographer's Dream' (Suzanne Vega)
While 'Ludlow Street' was straightforward in its meaning, 'Pornographer's Dream' relies on imagery and the ire of unmet expectations. 'She's a pornographer's dream,' the subject says, in the first verse. The narrator sums the situation up as futile.

'We are always dreaming of what we might be,' Vega sings. She won't be misled. She's aware that, like her friend, most of us will fail to achieve our goals, or will foolishly aim too high.

The song's protagonist has an unsettling persona: 'He is looking for women who are clothed and mysterious,' the narrator points out, 'Hidden in veils, dreaming in mystery.' But it is all beyond his reach; over his head.

Multi-instrumentalist Martin Slattery uses piano, reed and brass to create a decorative backdrop for this compelling, bossa nova.

'Frank & Ava' (Suzanne Vega)
Single release: US AAA: 20
'Frank and Ava' is a hot toddy of flavors, featuring Gerry Leonard's acoustic and electric guitar voicings and KT Tunstall's backing blends. Bassist Tony

Shanahan, then with The Patti Smith Group, hits all the right spots in this song about chemistry and incompatibility.

Singer and actor Frank Sinatra and American film actress Ava Gardner had a tempestuous relationship leading up to and during their 1951-1957 marriage. In this story-song about the stars, however, Vega opts to temper the topic with humor: 'On the way to the bidet is when the trouble used to start,' Vega narrates, intimating that the quarrels took shape on a constant basis. She finally concludes, 'that love was not enough' because the insecurities that plagued this glamorous Hollywood power couple were fodder to the press and never-ending.

'They needle till the jewels go raining down upon the ground,' was a nod to a much-publicized quarrel that the couple had the night before their wedding. According to *Frank the Voice* by James Kaplan, Sinatra and Gardner were staying at the Hampshire House having just returned from getting drinks with friends. The bellman delivered a letter that Gardner cautiously opened. It was from one of Sinatra's former lovers. Visibly upset, Gardner stood by the open window. 'Gritting her teeth, she pulled Frank's engagement ring – a six-carat emerald set in platinum, flanked with pear-cut diamonds – from her finger and threw it out into dark space.'

'She cool, it makes him cruel,' Vega sings flippantly. Gardner comes off as a jealous diva and Sinatra is anything but angelic. Vega's distillation of this Hollywood couple's story is entertaining and the arrangement suits her vocal range well.

'Edith Wharton's Figurines' (Suzanne Vega)

Kudos to Doug Yowell for tasteful percussion. Philip Sheppard's cello creates beautiful brush strokes in the final verse. But it's the theme that is the most curious. We know that Vega was an English major at Barnard and that she obsesses over certain authors. But why did Vega dedicate this song specifically to Wharton?

Wharton has often been seen as a feminist writer before her time. She won the Pulitzer Prize for *The Age of Innocence*, a novel which questions the ethics of 1870s New York society. Why *wouldn't* she be welcome in an album that defines New York?

In the third verse, Vega comments: 'See the portrait come to life.' She is referencing the portrait of a young girl, which inspired her award-winning novel.

But there's another female author barely hidden beneath the cracks, to whom Vega dedicated this song. New Yorker Olivia Goldsmith, author of *The First Wives Club*, died of complications from anesthesia during plastic surgery according to the *New York Post* in 2004. Vega feels the author's pain: 'Now, Olivia lies under anesthesia, her wit and wonder snuffed in a routine operation, her own beauty not enough.' Women, regardless of their age, era or income, often ache for beauty, even if it comes at a steep price. Vega's song points out the complexities.

'Bound' (Suzanne Vega)

In this searing look back at her marriage to Mitchell Froom, Vega sings, 'The way of the world has taken its toll,' but simultaneously declares her commitment: 'I am bound to you forever.' At the chorus, soul completely bared, she gives in to desperation: 'I am asking you, asking you if you might still want me.'

It's a heartbreaking song, bordering on depressing, but because the expressive words are surrounded by magical sonorous strings, courtesy of violinist Matthew Ward and cellist Philip Sheppard, there is a sense that the subject will somehow get through the miasma.

Graham Hawthorne serves as a veritable life force by using his aerobic drumming to provide a steadying shoulder, rather than a distraction. 'Bound' is well-supported by the talented ensemble and is the most cathartic track on the album – Vega's vocal performance is perceptively honest. This track required gumption.

'Unbound' (Suzanne Vega)

Using Mother Nature's flora as a muse, the subject gives a play-by-play as she unearths a plant by its tenacious roots. She feeds it and gives it sustenance, finally declaring its status as 'unbound.' In neat, linear phrases, Vega feeds our inquiring minds: 'I cut the twine and made it mine,' but the deeper story is just beginning to blossom.

Now, the subject looks back at her own life and notes a repetitive struggle. She, too, had been held back, compromised, 'confined with twine' in the midst of a destructive relationship. Vega proves once more how skillful she is at using metaphors within the confines of universally understandable language to get at human truths.

Leonard's driving riffs create a beguiling cacophony. Ruby Froom, Beccy Byrne and Emily Singer blend their mature voices to provide subtle backing vocals.

'As You Are Now' (Suzanne Vega)

In this acoustic fingerstyle guitar and string-laden love song to her daughter, Ruby Froom, Vega stops at nothing to illustrate her unconditional love: 'I will take up all your tears,' she begins. Beautiful orchestral interludes separate the verses and lead to the bridge, where the narrator hints at their future life together: 'Now I kiss your milky skin,' Vega sings, prior to the London Studio Orchestra's robust symphonic outro.

'As You Are Now' is written from the standpoint of a parent who cherishes and wants to hang on to the precious, fleeting days of childhood. Vega explains these sentiments in words that a child can fully understand and that a parent can lament or embrace.

Furthermore, the story is conveyed in a nursery rhyme-like meter, where the first two lines rhyme and the third and fourth lines follow suit. These simple elements combine to form an airy feeling of youthful innocence, which Vega echoes in her subtle vocal style.

'Angel's Doorway' (Suzanne Vega)

'She waits inside. Knows he's inside,' references the subject Angel's confused partner. Told in third-person, the story was inspired by Vega's brother-in-law, Angel Ruiz, a member of the New York City police force. The 'destruction' takes place at Ground Zero after the attack on The Twin Towers in New York City in 2001.

Angel has been besieged by 'the dust and the dirt and destruction.' Further along, Vega sadly intones how the chaos and violence affected her loved one: 'inside his brain is never the same.'

This is a haunting and realistic story which is lovingly sung. Vega's vocals are marvelously upfront. Gerry Leonard faithfully mirrors the bittersweet mood through driving rounds of electric and acoustic guitar. David Byrne drummer Graham Hawthorne resists any urge to woodshed and shows the necessary restraint this commemorative song deserves.

'Anniversary' (Suzanne Vega)

In commemoration of all those affected by the tragedy In New York, Vega wrote this sensitive tribute, with Leonard on reverberating guitar, Dixon on bass, Hawthorne on drums and Hogarth on acoustic guitar and percussion. Anthony Genn sings backing vocals.

Vega's vocals and acoustic guitar are perfectly matched. The mix is incredibly clear, you can hear fingers plucking back strings. The lyrics ooze with expression: 'Thick with ghosts, the wind whips round in circuitries.'

Vega's post-9/11 world is wracked with unpredictability. The droning melody acts as an evocative emphasis. The words in the verse rhyme and tell a story, but they're hard to decipher, perhaps in an effort to echo the confusion of the time – but the mood is, nevertheless, clear.

In the chorus, Vega sings with more solemnity – there has been a resolution of sorts, be it melancholy or otherwise: 'They meet you on each corner, they meet you on each street.'

'Obvious Question' (bonus track) (Suzanne Vega)

At 1:50, this song is frustratingly brief, given the mysterious title and that it's the closer. Vega explores the effects of alcohol on a male subject, which 'played upon his skin.' Sweetened with gorgeous strings and gentle guitar, Vega captures our interest but leaves us longing for more.

Tales from the Realm of the Queen of Pentacles (2014)

Personnel:
Suzanne Vega: vocals, guitar
Gerry Leonard: acoustic and electric guitars, harmonium
Larry Campbell: banjo, mandolin, cimbalom (1, 2, 8, 10)
Gail Ann Dorsey: bass (1, 2, 6, 8)
Tony Levin: bass (3, 5)
Mike Visceglia: bass (9, 10)
Zachary Alford: drums and percussion (1, 2, 6, 8)
Jay Bellerose: drums (3)
Sterling Campbell: drums (5, 9)
Doug Yowell: drums (1, 4, 7, 9, 10)
Joji Hirota: Taiko drums, shakuhachi (5, 6)
Alison Balsam: trumpet (10)
Catherine Russell: backing vocals (1, 2, 8, 9)
Smichov Chamber Orchestra, Prague (conducted by Josef Vondracek), strings (5, 6, 8)
Label: Amanuensis, Cooking Vinyl
Produced by Gerry Leonard at Clubhouse Studios, New York, Kyserike Station, New York, One East Studios, New York, Studio Disk, Barrandov (Prague), 18 February 2014
Additional technicians:
Michael Tudor: Andy Gilchrist: engineering, except Strings recorded at Studio Disk Barrandov, Prague by Lukas Vacek and Karel Holas. Trumpet recorded at Angel Recording Studios, London, Gary Thomas, additional recording: Kyserike Station, New York by Gerry Leonard
Release date: 18 February 2014
Highest chart places: UK (OCC): 37, US Folk Albums (Billboard): 5, US: 173
Running time: 36:40
Album Art: George Holz and Michael Tudor framed Vega in a tailored suit, crouching in front of archaic objects and an ancient archway, as she looks directly into the camera. Her smile is engaging, but mysterious.

Vega explained the meaning of her eighth album's title in an interview with the author in 2014.

> The pentacles are the suit for wealth and also the body and the material world. The songs are sort of spiritual songs about the body so they are stories, and they are also from the realm, the spiritual world, and how it interacts with the body, so that's why I chose the title.

According to the *Oxford Dictionary of Card Games*, Tarot card games originated in Italy and spread to most parts of Europe, but also were used in

Egypt and India. Accordingly, descriptions can vary. *Biddytarot.com* zeroes in on the characteristics of the 'queen' card as follows: 'The Queen of Pentacles represents prosperity and security.' The lyrics codify the royal's elite status.

As mentioned earlier, Vega had been dropped unexpectedly by Blue Note, leaving Vega with little time in which to rethink the next step in her trajectory. To her credit, she scrambled to start her own record label, which she entitled Amanuensis. *Dictionary.com* literally defines this term as 'a person employed to take dictation or to copy manuscripts.'

But Vega has explained in multiple interviews that her label name was actually a joke, pertaining to the idea of a servant getting to own the recording 'masters,' which was not reflective of the way recording studios operated when she first signed her own contract.

Vega also made the decision to work jointly with the artist-friendly Cooking Vinyl Label, out of South London. The company offered a unique deal in which artists would help finance their records initially, but then have the opportunity to reap considerably better royalties than they'd receive with a more traditional set-up.

Cooking Vinyl was formed in 1968 in the UK by former music manager and booking agent, Martin Goldschmidt, and former distribution manager Pete Lawrence. The label is acclaimed for creating 'artist services' deals whereby the artist maintains copyright ownership.

Cooking Vinyl has signed a long list of acts, including Billy Bragg, The Psychedelic Furs, The Pixies, and Beth Nielsen Chapman, among others.

CEO Martin Goldschmidt replied to questions about Suzanne Vega's professional relationship to the Cooking Vinyl Label in an interview with the author on 7 September 2022:

Suzanne was one of the artists that inspired me to start the label. Our second release was Michelle Shocked who was very much a contemporary of Suzanne in their heyday. Cooking Vinyl exists because we like working with unique and interesting artists and try to help the artist optimize the recording aspect of their career in line with their goals for success.

Mr. Goldschmidt elaborated on the process whereby the label works in conjunction with the artist's fanbase:

That is one of our big ups. We try to understand and enhance the artist-fan relationship and to help grow the fanbase through all our activities as part of 'team artist' (with the manager and the booking agent). This has worked really well for Suzanne.

Cooking Vinyl looks for the following qualities in their artists: 'Great music, intelligent music, an edge, and a fanbase.' The promotions were considerable and included an opportunity to order a signed setlist, one of 200 red vinyl

versions of the album, and a download of Vega singing the Lou Reed cover of
'Walk on the Wild Side.'

Mr. Goldschmidt emphasized that artists were involved in the promotions
and were made aware of how the promotional ideas were devised: 'Yes.
They were in collaboration with management and Suzanne,' he replied, and
added that Cooking Vinyl has 'a strong management team.' When asked what
promotions worked best, he remarked: 'All of them. It sold out very quickly.'

Cooking Vinyl's promotional team worked hand in hand with the artists:
'They were all discussed with and approved by management on behalf
of Suzanne. Mark Spector (label executive) has a great relationship with
Suzanne.'

Gerry Leonard, Lou Reed's producer, welcomed new sounds. The album
tracks were enhanced through a collaboration with the Prague Orchestra.

Producer Richard Barone worked alongside Vega in 2014 at the Lou Reed
Tribute Concert held in New York City. Were the album and live performance
connected in some mystical way? Barone replied:

It seems like I am always reunited with Suzanne in different ways. During
that time, we were both friends with Lou separately. I knew him separately.
She knew him differently than I did. I think the spiritual aspect of Lou
Reed had an impact on both of us. Knowing how Laurie Anderson (singer-
songwriter/Reed's wife) approached Lou's memorial services and things that
happened after, we were all brought to a very spiritual realm at that point.
That might have affected her, but I can't say for sure. We never talked about
that. But that period was a very spiritual period when Lou was a Buddhist or
interested in Tibetan Buddhism. And that was a big part of his sendoff when
he passed. We were both privy to that and all I can say is that definitely had
an impact on us.

Gerry Leonard, Michael Tudor and Vega jumpstarted sessions at the
Clubhouse Studio in July of 2013, along with drummer Zachary Alford and
bassist Gail Ann Dorsey. In August, the Smichov Chamber Orchestra added
strings.

But tracks, 'Don't Uncork What You Can't Contain' and 'Jacob and the Angel'
include less conventional instrumentation: Taiko drums and Shakuhachi flute
by Joji Hirota. Gerry Leonard talks about how decisions were made:

The sessions were done in blocks. I had done most of the preproduction
as we did our demos and writing. As part of this, we would suggest and
note any ideas for the songs. We got to book several days in Clubhouse
Studios and had a rotating cast of musicians come to get all the basic
tracking done and most of the vocals. When we decided that we wanted to
use strings on a number of songs, I decided to use my connection to the
Czech Republic through my friend Karel Holas from the Cechomor Band.

I knew that the quality of string players was very high and affordable in Prague, and in fact, we had previously done a tour with Suzanne, using a small orchestra there, so we had a good relationship with the orchestra and conductor. I went with the hard drives and a collection of arrangements and recorded strings. I also had become good friends with Joji Hirota and knew he also lived in Prague. I love his playing on Taiko drums and Shakuhachi flute and so I took the opportunity to integrate these elements into our arrangements.

'Crack in the Wall' (Suzanne Vega)

Zachary Alford shows great restraint in his role as drummer, kicking in strongly during the fine instrumental break, but otherwise paying close attention to the story. Bassist Gail Ann Dorsey's line pulls the elements together and Catherine Russell's light background singing adds just enough color and complement.

This song about transformation opens with a sense of marvel about the marred surface, but from a childlike perspective: 'I could not believe I found it.' But Vega's lyrical twists and turns make the song more of an adult undertaking, relying on a laid-back worldview to stir up interest. Vega's vivid action verbs bring an otherwise generic setting to life: 'a door sprang out around it.'

Leonard, on collaboration:

'Crack in the Wall' is a good example; Suzanne had a good start. She had the basic picking pattern and chords for the verse sections. She also had most of the lyric written. This is a song that we worked up in sound checks and perfected live before we brought it to the studio. I helped write the B part of the verse and put a musical interlude in the form of a guitar solo in. We were able to perfect the arrangement by playing it in front of audiences.

'Fools Complaint' (Suzanne Vega)

Vega has described the song live this way: 'It's the complaint of the fool who has no possessions and is free and is trying to leave that world.'

She has admitted to identifying with both the uppity Queen and the humble fool, which are both vital tarot cards, but which wield drastically different degrees of power.

This briskly animated guitar-driven song has an almost country flair. Gerry Leonard's production is impeccable, as Vega's voice is full and rich amid a bright array of instruments, and the harmonies are clear and sunny.

Vega describes the fool as 'that merry rootless man,' yet he remains in relatively good stead, as opposed to the Queen of Pentacles. Vega doesn't hold back when starting the story by declaring her hatred of the dreaded, self-serving monarch.

'I Never Wear White' (Suzanne Vega)
In an interview with the author on 19 June 2015, Vega discussed her decision
to request videos from fans who enjoyed singing this song:

> I was really struck by people saying, 'Oh, my six-year-old daughter was
> doing this in the kitchen the other day and it was so cute.' And I saw this
> film of this little girl singing 'I Never Wear White' and she put so much
> energy and attitude into it and a wide variety of people wrote to me saying
> that they really connect to that song. That's what I'm hoping to get, just the
> widest variety of human life. Everyone who writes to me saying that they
> really love that song. I really want to see you out there. I want to see you
> singing it.

It's logical that a native New Yorker would come up with this idea, with
black, smart casual garb being the *de riguer* uniform almost everywhere in
this fashion-conscious city, but Vega's voice digs more deeply into the subtext
than the title suggests.

'White is for virgins,' she smirks at the first verse, with a wink toward
societal judgments that historically influenced, not just feminine clothing
choice but cultural mores. Although in the second verse, she defends black,
the bona fide bad boy preferred by 'outlaws.' In the bridge, Vega makes an
all-out declaration, without the benefit of concrete examples, that black is the
truth and that all other colors lie.

Vega's crisp diction and a subtle hint of spite in her phrasing make the song
one of the album's highlights. Instrumentally, Leonard's effects glorify the
middle section. Leonard, on collaboration:

> This is another song in which we tried the 'try it out live' approach. The
> song had a different root. Suzanne had the lyric idea and needed a 'Rolling
> Stones' type riff. I keep a stockpile of ideas on my iPhone and had just come
> up with a more rock 'n 'roll riff. When Suzanne mentioned what she wanted,
> I said, 'Like this...?' and played the riff. She immediately started singing
> and we ended up writing that song very quickly. We had played with it in
> soundcheck, and one night in Seattle as an encore, Suzanne turned to me
> and said: 'Do you want to try the new one...?' We played it that night to a
> great reception and every night since I think.

'Portrait of the Knight of Wands' (Suzanne Vega)
In an interview with the author, Vega explained that the setting was:

> A beautiful, beautiful castle in Uppsala, Sweden. All that language on the
> bastions and the cannons, all that comes from the place that I was in on a
> particular day a couple of years ago. The place kind of spoke to me on that
> day. It's not something I seek out, but when I find myself there, I love it.

In this ancient-sounding tale, Vega captures that sense of beauty and mystery with a traditional rhyme scheme, a gentle finger-style accompaniment and a warm, breathy vocal performance.

She empathizes with the Knight's troubled state-of-mind, without revealing or holding too much back, but ultimately, she removes herself from the picture. At the short refrain, she imposes a few lines about technology, allowing us a brief moment in which to also time travel.

Ironically, and Vega would, of course, know this, the card is known for representing, in part, delayed travel. Was that interlude, then, an inside joke?

Vega presents a satisfying portrait of a multi-faceted, melancholy character, regardless of what time or space he is intended to occupy. Vega reveals her character's moods through her assessment of his body language: a 'sigh' or through 'thunder in his face' and when a nondescript bird enters the scene in the penultimate verse, the creature also vanishes in silence.

The extended electronic outro, which almost feels like it should belong to another track, allows for a surprise ending.

'Don't Uncork What You Can't Contain' (Suzanne Vega)
Leonard:

Suzanne had a strong outline for the lyrics and she also had the reference for the sample we ended up using and replaying. She knew she wanted an upbeat track and so I worked with her lyric and rhythmical vocal idea to come up with a guitar riff to suit the song. I ended up using a twelve-string acoustic guitar as it seemed to have the right sense of energy for the track. We kicked the ideas back and forth a bit until we arrived at the final version. We also used a slightly different layered approach. I temped out a lot of the track and we replaced things as we went along, like having Sterling Campbell come and play drums and do some drum programming.

Vega's first recorded sample was borrowed from rapper 50 Cent's Mid-eastern flavored 'Candy Shop', but she also relies on embellishments from the Prague Chamber Orchestra. Don't let the genie-in-the-bottle title mislead you – the story pertains to writing.

Joji Hirota, who was born in Japan, but relocated to London, achieved renown for merging Eastern and Western forms of instrumental music. His major works include: 'Rain Forest Dream', 'Tristan' and 'The Gate'. To further spice up Vega's upbeat cannon, Hirota played taiko drums on the track. (When performing live, Vega encourages hand claps). Tony Levin's rumbling bass and Leonard's magnetic riff also bear mention.

The song is a dizzying, rhythmic word salad that not every singer could pull off. Fortunately, Vega's command of diction and her natural ear for rhythm both work in her favor, and she, miraculously, makes her rendition sound effortless. That said, having the opportunity to do retakes in the studio may have given her confidence, but there's little to no safety net in the outside world. Vega explains the inherent challenge: 'It gets a good response live and it was very challenging to know all the lyrics and remember the melody. It's a little bit more complicated than some of the other songs.'

'Jacob and the Angel' (Suzanne Vega)
Vega describes the verses as a retelling of the story taken from the Bible (an episode from the book of Genesis), but as for the chorus, she told an audience that something weird happens: 'I, myself, am still trying to figure out what it is.'

So, the verses are straightforward, with Jacob either seeking the Angel's blessing, or the Angel threatening to flee, or the two futilely wrestling. However, come the chorus, Vega indemnifies 'this thing between us,' describing it the way one might describe a generic beast, with 'wings, horns and feathers,' etc. At this point, the Bible has left the building and Vega sounds like she's reciting a fanciful passage from Maurice Sendak's book, *Where the Wild Things Are.*

Instrumentally, Hirota casts an innovative spell with his taiko drums plus the traditional Japanese wooden flute, commonly known as the shakuhachi. Alford pops on both drums and percussion and Gail Ann Dorsey shines on bass; her melodic line is most forceful in the introductory measures. The leisurely, instrumental outro sounds as sonorous as whales communing beneath the sea.

'Silver Bridge' (Suzanne Vega)
Leonard's chunky introductory guitar riff gains traction before underlying Vega's exceptionally silky voice. It's in the first verse that we discover the sadness behind the title. 'Silver Bridge' is about death; Vega explicitly refers to the end of life with the term, 'the recently departed.'

In the second verse, an elderly man appears but turns away: 'on the stairway he ascended.' What is the lyrical response? 'I heard his struggle through the night with Saturn's hand extended.'

According to a popular, online mythology website, 'Death, particularly in old age, has been associated with Saturn since ancient times.' To that end, 'Silver Bridge' serves as a logical metaphor. But, as with much of Vega's material, nothing is simply cut and dried. Vega illustrates the passing of a life into death, not only through a Roman mythological lens, and not only through a believable, graying character, but through multiple poetic devices and the switching from third person in the verse to the more intimate second person in the chorus for emphasis.

It's also important to mention that Saturn's Roman equivalent in Ancient Greek mythology was Chronos, a god who was often depicted turning the zodiac wheel. Chronos is the personification of time prior to Socrates, and the rapid evaporation of time that Vega exploits in 'Silver Bridge' leaves a lasting and bittersweet impression.

At the chorus, when Vega commits to the about-face, she shies away from profound narrative long enough to pose a direct question: 'Are you standing on that bridge? Which way are you facing?' Death was battling with the old man but now lurks behind our threshold.

In the next verse, the narrator stands frozen. Is she, too, afraid of the inevitable ending of life? Is she standing dangerously close to the silver bridge?

The narrator is startled by 'a light of silver.' And as if to underscore impending danger, Leonard's hurdy-gurdy harmonium casts a spell on the following measures.

When Vega resumes her singing, she questions her role. Is she an observer from a safe distance or should she get involved? She rehashes the experience and describes her further action as 'a kind of vigil keeping.' There's a sanctity to the old man's passing; a ceremonial protocol.

Back at the chorus, there's full-blown orchestration. The topic is recycled: 'Are you standing at the bridge? Which way are you facing?' Without further explanation, and after more dynamic strums, the repetition of the first verse suffices. The story's been told.

Coincidentally, The Silver Bridge was an actual American structure that spanned the Ohio River, and which fell apart in 1967. American author Gray Barker suggested that there is a credible link between the bridge and the paranormal. What were Vega's songwriting intentions? Was the elderly man a ghost?

'Song of the Stoic' (Suzanne Vega)

Vega imagined the subject of this song as being 'a similar character as 'Luka', maybe years later.' This older version of 'Luka' has to contend with an aggressive father: '18 years of pain upon my body to the bone,' goes the disheartening story.

In predominantly strophic form, the contrasting section consists of 'oohs' and no lyrics. A man looks back at his life, recounting his livelihood and failed luck at marriage; the object of his affections was already taken, but they remained friends.

It took Vega twelve well-crafted verses to tell this story, and similarly to 'The Queen and the Soldier', the songwriter intones a multitude of lines that emphatically move the story forward, but with no fat on the bone.

Like-minded readers, Leonard and banjoist Larry Campbell, feed off each other's energies. It's less a showdown, more a meeting of intuitive minds. Members of The Smichov Chamber Orchestra Prague weave legato lines into the right spaces, creating sweeping crescendos and subtle resolutions.

'Laying on of Hands/Stoic 2' (Suzanne Vega)

Ushered in by a cluster of drums and garage rock guitar, Vega ponders the plight of Mother Theresa and the power of 'touch as a language.' In a

YouTube video, she expresses that touch can be 'loving or painful' and that she hopes it can be received as healing.

The song settles in with a jangly chord progression that triggers flashbacks of early Jefferson Airplane. Alford is selective about his drum fills, but they're worth the wait. Catherine Russell, who has sung backing vocals in sessions with Roseanne Cash, Steely Dan, David Bowie, Gloria Estefan, among others, exceeds expectations with her powerful pipes. Over the course of a couple of bars, Russell reaches an impressive fever pitch. Check her out on the 2016 album, *Harlem on My Mind*.

When Vega sings 'oohs' in the chorus, the instrumentalists explode. Who knew Mother Theresa could inspire such a rollicking tribute? 'The thing about a Stoic is that he's always understated,' Vega concludes.

This full-on jam session shows off the individual members of the studio band, but the players lay low when Vega asserts her cool demeanor. Leonard clarifies why he used two drummers:

> We were looking for a strong rhythmic element for this song. I had used the two-drummer approach before, and it seemed like the right fit for this song. Also, Sterling (Campbell) and Doug (Yowell) are good friends but different in approach and style. I felt like I could get a great performance by combining the two.

'Horizon (There is a Road)' (Suzanne Vega)

Vega dedicated this song to Vaclav Havel, the first elected president of the Czech Republic, who was, in addition, a highly acclaimed playwright, memoirist and essayist.

In an interview with the author on 19 June 2015, Vega elaborated on her relationship with Havel and how his admirable characteristics inspired the song.

> I had the privilege to know Vaclav Havel a bit in the last years of his life and we had a friendship, which was so lovely. He gave me a copy of his book *To the Castle*, and he would come out to the shows and we would chat a little bit and I really, really liked him. I liked him for what he achieved, I liked him for his intellect and his humor and the fact that he was a playwright and also the president of his country. It was great. What I say in the song 'Horizon' is, he is someone who has lived his life in the spirit of love even though I think he suffered incredibly when he was in jail, he suffered physically, emotionally and mentally, but he was able to maintain his integrity and come out and not only survive but lead a country into freedom, which is so remarkable, and do it with grace and honor, without a punishing energy. He didn't turn around and say, 'we're going to punish all these Communists.' It was like, 'No, we're moving forward.' And I found all of this to be very inspiring and that's what I hope to encapsulate in that song.

Leonard's guitar leads Vega in and keeps up the momentum; Alison Balsom's unexpected trumpet solo propels the song to new heights.

Vocally, Vega's admiration for her Czech friend shines through with each carefully crafted lyric and delicate phrase. It's not easy to express a stone-cold loyalty without sounding maudlin, but Vega managed to do so. Near the end, she sings the tag an octave higher, and although her head voice is relatively thin in contrast to her chest voice, the shift works – her vulnerability creeps through.

Lover, Beloved: Songs from an Evening with Carson McCullers (2016)

Personnel:
Suzanne Vega: vocals, composer
Duncan Sheik: composer, Hammond B3, harmonium, pedal bass, percussion, background vocals
Gerry Leonard: arranger, guitar, mandolin, producer, ukulele, vibraphone
Roswell Rudd: trombone
David Rothenberg: clarinet, bass clarinet
Michael J. Merenda Jr.: banjo, banjo-ukulele
Jason Hart: piano
Will Holshouser: accordion
Byron Isaacs: double bass
Yuvall Lyon: drums
Doug Yowell: percussion
David Poe: background vocals
Ruby Froom: background vocals
The Garrison Gang: background vocals
Kevin Killen: mixing
Bob Ludwig: mastering
Michael Tudor: engineer
Milo Decruz: engineer
Label: Amanuensis/Cooking Vinyl
Produced by Gerry Leonard at Sneaky Studios, Garrison, New York on 14 October 2016
Release date: 14 October 2016
Highest chart places: UK: Did not chart, US Folk Albums (Billboard): 22
Running Time: 33:02
Album Art: Mirroring her muse, Carson McCullers, Vega sits on a stoop with legs akimbo, one arm resting on her chin, and a cigarette dangling between two fingers. To complete the visual profile, she boasts a brunette, chin-length 'pageboy' cut and fringe. The dark, tailored suit and sneakers reflect McCullers'ss androgynous nature.

Why was Suzanne Vega, a contemporary, dyed-in-the-wool New Yorker so smitten with the personality and writings of American southern novelist Carson McCullers? And beyond that, what made Vega believe that McCullers'ss work would not only inspire an occasional song, but an entire musical, which would be named, *Carson McCullers Talks About Love*?

As mentioned earlier, Vega's obsession with McCullers began at Barnard College, where, fittingly, as an English major, Vega based a project on several profound McCullers stories. Fortunately, she found her co-writing partner in crime when developing an artistic relationship with Tony award-winning,

American composer and pop/folk sensation, Duncan Sheik, years later. This union gave Vega and Sheik an optimum opportunity to expand their audience. At that juncture, of course, Vega had the wherewithal to go full throttle, through storytelling, studio work and live performance. She would no longer be subjected to grades or collegial judgments. Consequently, when invited back to perform the show at her alum, Barnard College, she was a raving success.

In an interview with the author on 8 November 2016, Vega explained her fascination with the Southern writer:

I just think she's a really interesting, modern person. She was way ahead of her time. Her androgyny, her bisexuality, and the way she used language was very tough and feels very contemporary to me. And the way she continued working, even though she had all of these disabilities. She was very able, in spite of all her illnesses, and her attitude towards the way she was, able to write, from a very empathic point of view, especially in *The Heart is a Lonely Hunter*, her first novel.

McCullers was a complex, but consistently imaginative author. At the age of nineteen, she published her first short story, 'Wunderkind'. In 1917, when she published *The Heart is a Lonely Hunter*, she magnified the lives of small-town misfits and received critical acclaim.

Similarly to Vega, who switched courses from dance and literature to songwriting and performance, McCullers abandoned her first love, which was music, for literature. Despite cultural differences, Vega and McCullers seemed to be cut from a similar cloth. They both started their creative careers early on, exhibited great ambition, showed resilience as artisans, and boldly explored their respective themes, even when these themes triggered controversy.

Vega first discovered McCullers when, as a teen, she read the short story 'Sucker'. In a promotional video, she explains how the storyline affected her: 'There are kids who really have it rough and are struggling to dream and to make a life for themselves and that feels very universal.'

It's not a stretch, then, to see how deeply Vega connected to 'Sucker'. Although, unlike Vega, the characters lived in a small town, they were desperate to find themselves despite all odds. After all, in some ways, Vega could have been a central character, as her own struggle often mirrored the intensity of McCullers'ss upended youngsters.

By shaping her ideas into a musical, of course, Vega had to make specific choices. As such, when illustrating the author's hot and cold temperament, she balanced out fury and feistiness with humor and grace.

Leonard judiciously selected session musicians who played everything from trombone and upright bass to ukulele, and with the expertise of established musical writer, Duncan Sheik, her wheelhouse became a provocative blend of blues, jazz, burlesque and literature.

This album was markedly different from previous studio albums for a variety of reasons. First of all, Vega had an opportunity to explore the blues, the genré which originated in McCullers'ss southern neck-of-the woods.

Secondly, Vega returned to her college acting days, by inhabiting a central character for the duration of the project, something she'd not done before, and which she considered to be 'thrilling.' In addition to showcasing blues, she was able to honor McCullers's own piano-playing trajectory, through Sheik's unique keyboard-driven arrangements.

In a YouTube interview with Australian CNN entertainer reporter Shanon Cook, Vega explained that the album was based on the two-hour original musical *Lover, Beloved: Songs from an Evening with Carson McCullers*, co-written with Sheik. The show premiered in Houston, Texas at Rattlestick Theater in 2018.

Cook asked Vega about the historical role of women in music. Had Vega encountered discrimination as a female artist? What was her take? Vega took the answer to heart and shared pertinent ancestral information. When she discovered that her paternal grandmother had been a drummer in the 1930s in an all-female band, she recognized the vast historical influence of women in music yet stressed that she didn't feel gender played a particularly strong role in her own trajectory.

Vega has often stated in interviews that she saw McCullers as being ahead of her time; the southern writer clearly followed a long line of other female artists, who, despite not being advertised as influential in popular culture, thereafter, co-existed and thrived, despite often being perceived as marginal according to societal norms. Duncan Sheik:

Suzanne and I are both Buddhists and we share the same specific practice of Buddhism. We were sort of in each other's orbit.

Suzanne can be sort of shy sometimes. We would connect in some brief way but then Gerry Leonard started playing guitar with her; Gerry had been my guitar player almost since the beginning of my career and so Suzanne and I kept having this connection with each other.'

After *Spring Awakening* happened, Suzanne's daughter, Ruby, was a big fan and Suzanne was forced to listen to that annoying soundtrack over and over again and she said, 'maybe I should call Duncan and we can work on these Carson McCullers songs together.' It was about 2009-2010 when the bulk of the work happened.

I had already written *Whisper House*. You can say, I was more in theater mode at that point, so it was a good time to connect.

There were several workshops: one at the Rattlestick in New York, one in Martha's Vineyard, a very fancy place to do a workshop, and one in Empac, Troy, New York, which is an incredibly well-funded college. It's sort of in the middle of nowhere but it was a good experience.

And we also had a week or two at Harvard at Cambridge. We had these nice situations where we got to work on this together for a week or two. That was a lot of fun.

We spent a lot of time together. I personally am not the kind of person who likes to sit in a room with somebody else and write stuff. It was more that Suzanne would send me lyrics and I would create some kind of musical concept for those lyrics, and we would go from there.

With my understanding of Carson's history and the time frame in which she was writing, it's kind of like this process of layering music from the '40s and '50s and layering that with Suzanne's oeuvre and my own sensibility. So, it's taking all of these things into consideration and then saying, 'What is that gumbo?' for lack of a better word.

I had a little bit of a connection with Carson McCullers myself when I was in high school. I went to boarding school in New England and I had a cool literature teacher. There were some McCullers's texts in that class. This idea really hit me hard, this idea of the lover and the beloved. There's one person who is always going to be the lover in the sense that they're always going to be unrequited and there's always this person that's going to be the beloved. There's this person that loves them that they don't love them back. It's binary, and that's really what the concept is.

For a seventeen-year-old boy who is always in these unrequited love situations, that was really terrifying and powerful and I was hoping that it wasn't really true, but it seemed true.

There's eroticism and then there's another kind of love that is a pure appreciation – agape love. I think, Carson clearly always struggled with this thing, of having these weird, and probably not particularly fulfilling, romantic dalliances and then longing for a purer relationship, like a platonic ideal of love.

Sheik explained the nature of their collaboration:

Suzanne's a great lyricist and it wasn't really my role in that situation. I think she was looking for me to give her musical material so she could tell the story and write lyrics. It was a little vulcanized in terms of who was doing what, as opposed to Rodgers and Hammerstein. Again, we did a workshop sometime in 2009 and then there was the production in Houston in 2018 or 2019 so that was a period, of say, eight years, where there was a decent amount of back and forth. These things evolved over time and there were a couple of different directions involved in the show throughout the process. The thing about musical theater, it's kind of a dumb cliché, musical theater shows are never finished, they just close at some point.

Sheik's role in the production:

I would do these demos that had very specific musical ideas that would then be incorporated into the record and it was recorded in the house that I lived in at the time in Garrison, New York, so there were a lot of funny instruments and stuff. But it was Gerry's job to produce; I wasn't there the whole time but they made the record at my place. Suzanne was really driving the train on the narrative aspect and the lyrical aspect, and the different directors had different ideas about how the story might be structured. It ended up with this scenario, wherein the production of the play, the first act was when McCullers was younger and she's giving a talk, and the second act was toward the end of her life, so the first act was her first flush of fame and the second act was about this person who was flaming out in a tragic way. So that was all the doing of Suzanne and the directors of the production. I was obviously honored to be asked to be a part of it. It's great that it lives on in its way. It's fascinating to see what people still remain interested in. Some things are big for a minute and fall away. It becomes compelling over a decade or two so it's cool to become part of something like that.

'Carson's Blues' (Suzanne Vega, Michael Jefry Stevens)

How does one combat cruel name-calling? Especially when it escalates. Maybe one can ignore the relatively tame taunt that you're 'a wounded sparrow,' but what if you're typecast as 'a devilish bitch?'

The very human response, 'I'm an iron butterfly' signals that the victim can view life through two distinctive lenses and that she has a precarious nature: 'I can be sweet and charming and suddenly switch.' The phrase 'iron butterfly' (no reference to the rock band) suggests a tough core inside a delicate form. To elaborate on the main character's vulnerability, Vega as Carson McCullers laments, 'I've never belonged.'

Vega carefully deconstructs McCullers's temperament, and then, I believe, it's up to us to decide who's fair and who isn't. Is the author a social misfit or a tender soul in need of mercy?

'Carson's Blues' is a co-write with a swing. It's a song that, on the surface, doesn't take itself too seriously, yet serves the purpose of gently illuminating McCullers's imagined interior voice.

The B section: 'I talk to strangers, strangers, strangers one at a time,' appears, at first, to be a non-sequitur, story-wise, yet musically, the phrase fits in well with the tempo and Vega's sultry delivery. I believe, too, that she intentionally uses the poetic device of repetition with the word 'strangers' to acknowledge McCullers's social anxiety.

That section ushers in an intricate keyboard solo and 'Big Easy' horn. Vivacious brass frames Vega's vocals for a clean-cut ending. This charming romp features Leonard's masterful guitar.

'New York is My Destination' (Suzanne Vega, Duncan Sheik)

'All of the tales of seduction' come together via 'glitterati' and 'paparazzi.' With a nod to the great American Songbook, Vega envisioned 'an old-fashioned, Rodgers and Hammerstein kind of quality.'

Sheik's instrumental preparation work involved an ES-175 electric guitar and a smattering of 7th and 9th chords punched out on organ. Vega, too, punches out the lyrics; not in a Broadway-centric belt, or as a Sinatra-style crooner, but in a highly-energized way. She inhabits the inherent rhythm of the quickly moving phrases, with the savoir-faire of a ballroom-dancing contestant on a televised reality show.

Predictably, Vega was inspired by her native city's charms and envisioned McCullers enjoying all that it offers. She has drawn much of her material from her surroundings, but some songs trump others; 'New York is My Destination' contains all of the classic ingredients and ranks with other notable 'place songs': 'I Left My Heart in San Francisco', 'Moonlight in Vermont' or 'April in Paris' in terms of structural unity, a focused, heartfelt message and a contagious melody. Vega has proclaimed: 'I think the character of New York comes out in the characters.' Sheik recollected the setting:

I'm pretty sure we were in Martha's Vineyard for that one particular workshop there. They put us up in a humble house that happened to have an organ from the mid-1960s. I was like, 'let me come up with some idea,' with this silly organ in this random house in Martha's Vineyard.

'Suzanne has a great sense of humor,' he explained. 'With a roll of the eyes she said, 'Oh, Mitchell,' he was always playing with his organ' (in reference to Mitchell Froom). Sheik also recalled:

The DNA of a few of these songs was coming from Gerry Leonard who was very involved in that project as well. I had some musical ideas and Gerry had some musical ideas. They kind of fused together in some way and Suzanne had her own ideas. And there were a few of these songs that she had written at Barnard, I guess. There were a few of these very nascent ideas that ended up finding their way into the show and into the record. It was collaborative between Gerry, Suzanne and myself. (Credited Michael Jefry Stevens was Vega's musical advisor at Barnard).

'Instant of the Hour After' (Suzanne Vega, Duncan Sheik)
In an interview with the author, I asked Vega about this couplet: 'How I love you, how I loathe you.' Why such ambivalence?

That was written from a story that she wrote, 'Instant of the Hour After' – those words are right from her story, the story of two alcoholics who are drinking and at the end of the night, they are having this argument. It's pretty obvious it's the way you feel if you love someone who drinks; you feel ambivalent, I think.

Against a tableau of mesmerizing, rolling piano, Vega reframes McCullers's story, written during her years at Columbia University, with an astounding range of emotion. In a related video, Sheik compared the brooding theme to a Virginia Woolf story. It's a troubling, well-interpreted premise. Sheik:

> There's definitely a Kurt Weill thing going on in that. Someone had been discussing working with me on a trilogy of Brecht plays at CSC, which is a really cool downtown theater that I did ultimately do, but I was a little bit immersed in this mode of some Kurt Weill music and so I think it came out of that energy. It was circulating in my brain at that moment. And Kurt Weill was a contemporary of Carson's, so it felt appropriate to be quoting that subject.

Harmonically, Sheik draws in the listener through dizzy chordal changes, but then mystifyingly returns to the tonic. The melody is equally suspenseful; Vega, exploring a thematic sense of despair, breathes pain and life into the held notes, and still in character, exhales with ennui. Sheik examines McCullers's plight:

> There was her alcoholism and the alcoholism of her erstwhile husband. For sure, that was her undoing, and there were a lot of people in her environment. Alcohol abuse was very rampant in that era, especially among writers. And they probably got some benefit from it on some level and it killed them.

'We of Me' (Suzanne Vega, Duncan Sheik)
In an interview with the author, Vega spoke frankly about being an outsider:

> Well, I myself felt like a kind of outsider growing up. I had a different father from the rest of my brothers and sisters and I was raised in a neighborhood that was mostly black and Puerto Rican, so I stood out in a way, not in a good way, either. So, I suppose I identify with that role.

'All other people have a 'we' to claim...,' she sings. With moving backing vocals on the chorus, Vega zeroes in on the theme of emotional isolation and its damning residual effects.

In a promotional YouTube video along with Sheik, Vega admitted that this was written practically overnight. Sheik had an arrangement 'in his pocket' that 'didn't have a home.' He considered the song to be the most 'contemporary' song on the album.

Vega mirrored the song after McCullers's short story, 'A Member of the Wedding' and claimed that McCullers 'frequently found herself involved with two people at once.' The song is probably the most commercial track on the album, with its steady beat and engaging rhymes.

'Annemarie' (Suzanne Vega, Duncan Sheik)
'Annemarie' required Vega to take another deep dive into McCullers'ss fascinating backstory. In an interview with the author published in 2016

in *pennyblackmusic*, Vega discussed the factors that influenced this heartbreaking song:

> 'Annemarie' was someone that Carson McCullers was in love with, and from reading her biography, she worshipped her. If you look up the woman, Annemarie Clara Schwartzenbach, she was loved by many people, not just Carson McCullers, so in the song she raises Annemarie to the point of being a kind of deity, especially by the last verse. She's kind of both a real person and a kind of icon.

Vega gets to the heart of the matter when interpreting the targeted prose in this story song about a high-stakes affair, and where there is obviously much to lose given the era. The lines are palpable and fatalistic: 'I knew you'd haunt me for the rest of my life,' she sings. The affair was thrilling and, at times, even frightening. That romantic drama is exacted through the use of hyperbole, as well as stark, realistic statements.

In the promotional video for the album, Vega claimed that Sheik encouraged her to extend her vocal range on this ballad – she tackled the high register with an impressive confidence. Sheik:

> 'Annemarie' was a super-aristocratic German morphine addict who Carson became infatuated with. A lot of these quote-unquote relationships that Carson had were like figments of her own imagination. She knew these people; she hung out with them, but in her own mind, she was in a relationship with them. And these people were like crazy characters who were floating through the environment.

As a songwriting duo, Vega and Sheik were a commendable match. Sheik admired Vega's penchant for allowing the lyrics to express and anticipate emotions, as opposed to using her voice to deliberately create a dramatic effect.

'12 Mortal Men' (Suzanne Vega, Duncan Sheik)
This musical covers a myriad of styles and moods, but '12 Mortal Men' is one of the most sobering numbers. Set against a swamp-filled background, Vega literally whispers the grim narration. Remarkably, the bleak story is conveyed with a great deal of detail through the efficiency of merely three verses.

'Where I come from there's poverty… Nobody comes here. Nobody leaves,' the narrator warns us. The hushed vocal quality will make more sense when we hear the second verse; the characters have reason to live in fear and mistrust their neighbors.

Vocally, Vega remains very cognizant of dynamics throughout. In fact, were the story not told in whispers, danger could lie ahead. Again, she uses repetition to grab our attention.

The grim theme centers around a 'chain gang', a phenomenon that existed in the American South, and which can best be described as a group of male prisoners who perform hard labor on the road. For added security, the convicts are conjoined by ankle chains, hence the name.

The town in which this setting takes place has a library, and while such a building wouldn't generally trigger discomfort, it does in this case because the library houses shocking content; among the racks of pedestrian books, patrons can access an actual 'whipping report'.

Despite their fruitless lot-in-life, however, the prisoners manage to rejoice, hence: 'Twelve mortal men in a song of liberty.' 'In my heart I see a crowd,' the narrator states in the final verse. Despite such dire circumstances, the men imagine a world of harmony, where 'each one is loved.' Sheik:

I grew up in South Carolina, so I have an understanding of the energy of the history of that place, this idea of a place that oppressed black men. They wouldn't have been slaves, but for all intents and purposes, they still would have been in a position of slavery. They were imprisoned by the state and they were made to work in a slave-like fashion. I was trying to get at the idea of the blues from the '40s and '50s. That was definitely what I was trying to get at.

Sheik discusses the 2022 film, *Elvis*, directed by Baz Lurhmann:

There's a lot that's fascinating about it, especially the sound design, production design, how the music sounds, and the way he was juxtaposing the black music culture of that place and time, with the white music culture of that place and time. That's very much what I was trying to evoke, a similar kind of energy. On *Brother, Where Art Thou*, there's an energy about that music that is really specific; it's not the cliché thing, 'oh, it's about the blues,' but that eerie other thing from which cliché blues emanates. I was trying to get that deep, deep blues energy. Where does that come from?

'Harper Lee' (Suzanne Vega, Duncan Sheik)
Carson McCullers wasn't above making catty comments about her successful literary peers. To that end, the team made use of poetic license. Vega pooled certain applicable quotes and crafted them neatly into a set melodic and rhythmic scheme.

'She has more to say than Hemingway' was likely the most humorous line, as Hemingway is often known for his spare narratives. Proust ('Believe me, Proust goes on and on and on for several volumes...'), Faulkner and Fitzgerald barely escape unscathed.

At the chorus, Vega liberates us from the barbs and queries and gets downright direct: 'Why do they always compare her to me?'

The takeaway is that McCullers was competitive with other writers, but especially with Harper Lee, the famed author of *To Kill a Mockingbird*. As such, Vega configured a tongue-in-cheek response to McCullers's one-upmanship. In an interview with the author, Vega revealed:

The line about 'My sad café is greater than his Gatsby' – someone else said it online, and I thought she (McCullers) would have liked it. So, she didn't actually say it, but I thought she would have liked it, and the final line, 'I'd like to kill more than your mockingbird,' was actually written by Duncan Sheik, who wrote the music, and it was such a great line that I had to grab it and throw it right in there, and it rhymed and everything. That's the one line she did not say, but the rest of it is pretty much taken from her autobiography.

Sheik:

I didn't do any lyrics at all, although Suze does credit me with one particular line in the 'Harper Lee song – it's a really catty line. That particular song was all about her competitiveness with Harper Lee and finding a way of expressing Carson's annoyance. Who is this other woman who is taking my place right now? This person took her place on some level. Sometimes you get annoyed when people who are your colleagues get more popular in the public consciousness. They leapfrog you. Why does this guy deserve this? I'm the one who has the goods. But it's silly because that's just a thing that happened.

'Lover, Beloved' (Suzanne Vega, Duncan Sheik)
The title song is a truly tender ballad. A few Debussy-like, up-tempo piano notes, which double in time, set the stage, after which point, a dreamy tempo kicks in. In the verse, Sheik's piano line closely couches Vega's gentle voice.

In the chorus, there is a change of focus; simple chords frame Vega's lead vocals. They ring out and take center stage. A percussive, ambient instrumental foreshadows her re-entrance. The second instrumental, however, includes aggressive brass.

Although the title suggests a song of pure devotion, the content of the verse belies that notion. 'Lover, Beloved' is, in some ways, a tragic story: 'Each bears the burden of loving too much,' Vega ruminates.

But emotions run hot and cold. At the bridge, there is a sense of positivity, of coming together, when Vega croons: 'man across the sticks will be lovers for eternity.'

'The Ballad of Miss Amelia' (Suzanne Vega, Michael Jefry Stevens)
In an interview with the author, Vega explains:

That is the storyline and plot of 'The Ballad of the Sad Café'. All I did was adapt it. That's the one I wrote in college. There's a longer version, actually, so that was the shorter version. I found it a pleasure to take her work and adapt it. Her writing itself is quite musical because she was a trained musician and I think sometimes her cadences and rhythms crept in there, so it was fairly easy to adapt.

'The Ballad of Miss Amelia' is about the title character's loveless marriage to Marvin Macy. A secondary character is a 'little hunchback.' The arrangement is laced with amusing instrumental starts and stops, and with nods to burlesque, New Orleans jazz and the blues.

It's not an easy song to sing, as there is a lot of innuendo and humor in the story, which requires some act-outs, but Vega viscerally inhabits this way-out woman, vocally and emotionally. She shows great affection for the character she's portraying; she probably internalized them after steeping herself in McCullers's vivid stories, which this time around include lots of wisecracks. Sheik:

Part of it was trying to conjure up my own sense of a certain time and how the music might sound at that time, like an Edward Hopper painting. What was the imaginary song that was coming out of the radio in that diner in that painting? Suzanne has very specific ideas about what she wants to sing, but she's so open to things musically. It was awesome to be able to express a bunch of ideas, and then she put them and made them her own. There didn't need to be a lot of fretting about the specifics of things. She wrote lots of compelling, lyrical ideas and I wrote some music and she made it her own.

'Carson's Last Supper' (Suzanne Vega, Duncan Sheik)
The title may bring to mind the last supper of Christ before the crucifixion, but 'Carson's Last Supper' is, in actuality, an imagined feast with Carson McCullers acting as hostess. McCullers died well before her time at the age of 50 from a stroke. But what was her legacy? How would she have liked to have been remembered?

'Carson's Last Supper' is a celebration of life, despite all of its messy obstacles. It's a plea for inclusivity, a table at which all are encouraged to break bread.

After Sheik's simple but brisk piano introduction, Vega sings: 'I love the world, sometimes it loves me. The love of my life is humanity.' Here, she looks beyond the boundaries of the ego by offering her body of work to posterity. When she mentions, 'humanity,' I believe she's making a value judgment, that universal love for our fellow man is preferential to mere romantic love.

In the next verse, she celebrates the 'rich and the poor' – and we can draw parallels between the characters in her novels and short stories and humans that dog-eared her pages.

In the chorus, Vega's voice exudes a special warmth, as if she and Sheik purposely wrote each note of the beautiful spiraling melody to suit her range. The message couldn't be plainer: 'Come and sit at this table.' Although the idea of sequencing tracks may be a thing of the past, it really made so much sense here. 'Carson's Last Supper' is a perfect closer. Sheik:

In that song, in particular, this is where Suzanne and my Buddhist faith come into play because there's this idea of a common bond of all humanity. It's a really important central idea. And it was something that, I think, Carson McCullers was longing for really earnestly in her writing and did not find.

Live Albums

Suzanne Vega: Live in London 1986

Personnel:
Suzanne Vega: vocals and guitar
Mitchell Froom: instrumental arrangements
Michael Visceglia: bass
Garo Yellin: cello
Aaron Heick: clarinet, oboe,
Charlie Giordano: piano, accordion
Thom Cadley: Recording Engineer, Mixer
Roy Simmons, Brian Vibberts, Ryan Hewitt: Assistant engineers
Kevin Hartmann: House sound mixer
Ira Malek: mixer
Label: A&M
Recorded: 27 April 1986
Released: October 1986
Highest Chart Rank: AUS: 93

'Left of Center' (featuring Joe Jackson) and **'Left of Center'** (Charlie Giordano)

UK: 32, US AAA: 35, IRE: 28

I was happy to see that 'Left of Center' found a home in the Vega oeuvre. Yes, it fared significantly well commercial-wise on the *Pretty in Pink* soundtrack, but the song deserved to be, as it is here, part and parcel of another commercial work.

The *Pretty in Pink* score recording featured an outstanding guest keyboardist, Joe Jackson, whose 'Steppin' Out' had been a Top Ten hit in 1982. Jackson played a big part in the second wave of the American British Invasion. Because so much of Vega's studio work centered on guitar, the addition of Jackson's ivories was compellingly one-off.

Here, Charlie Giordano tackles the keyboard arrangement and does an excellent job, although some Jackson fans might insist that he created the pianistic blueprint when recording for the *Pretty in Pink* soundtrack. But he's a heavy hitter. Giordano replaced Danny Federici in Bruce Springsteen's E Street Band and also worked with vocalist Pat Benatar.

It was a song originally designated for film, and that almost missed the deadline, but Addabbo and Vega ultimately rallied to the cause. Co-writer Steve Addabbo was there when the song was, not only conceptualized but hatched and released into the world. In an interview with the author on 9 June 2022, Addabbo explained how the co-write landed on the *Pretty in Pink* soundtrack.

We're on the road after the first record. I was still on the road with them in an RV somewhere in Northern California, Suzanne was on a gig. A&M said we have a new soundtrack coming out and we'd like you to contribute. So, they sent Suzanne the script and we were hoping for a demo. We were in San Francisco on a Monday. I asked: 'Have you looked at the script yet?' She says, 'No. It was a silly script.' I asked her to just scribble something. She's writing something. Finally, I ask, 'Do you have anything?' and she said no, but I saw something down in the corner that she had scribbled: 'left of center.' I told her that I liked that phrase and asked her, 'Why don't you use that?'

Suzanne wrote more lyrics, but Addabbo was getting restless. He explained:

We're supposed to deliver a demo on Thursday and it's now Monday or Tuesday. We're driving to L.A. and I say, 'We'll just sit in your room and we'll see if I can help you finish this song.'

I go down there with my guitar and start playing what would become the opening lick. We develop the idea and finish the song in about two hours. She had a lot of lyrical and melodic ideas. Thursday, we go to A&M Studios. I hadn't even worked out all the chords in the bridge yet, but she sang it and they liked it, and gave us a recording budget. They also said, 'How about having Joe Jackson play piano?'

Of course, we said, 'Why not?' We handed the recording in and the soundtrack was really rocking. Ours, though, was still kind of acoustic. Suzanne liked the demo, though, and because it was Suzanne, I didn't think we needed the big drum sound.

But they said, 'Why don't you have Arthur Baker do a remix?' So, Arthur did the big drum sound and really finished the song. and we ended up with this version on the soundtrack. It's my only co-write with Suzanne but it's done well.

When we went to the opening, we were all excited as we waited for the song. There's this one scene where the character is in her bedroom doing homework and listening to the radio and the song comes on. We thought it would feature later in the movie but it never came back. We were a little crestfallen walking out of the movie, but we were on the soundtrack and that went platinum so that's okay. I'm glad they made us beef it up because we were on the same soundtrack as The Psychedelic Furs.

It was a magical time. I was just trying to get out of the studio as a tech and Suzanne; we just came together at the right time in our careers.

Richard Levine directed the 1986 'Left of Center' video. He worked on The Smiths' 'How Soon Is Now?' a year earlier. Levine created similarly contemporary visuals for Lionel Ritchie.

The video features close-ups of both Jonathan Gordon's wildly jagged electric guitar solo, and a glamorously made-up Vega, either shot under bright lights or in the shadows. Her lucid tones are, at times, almost robotic, in keeping, most likely, with the new wave era.

The lyrics, which reel with inner-city sensations, also synched up perfectly with the closeups of Vega, donning black leather, as Joe Jackson's ivories extend through the outro. The striking MTV video has attracted approximately three million fans.

As Addabbo intimated, with the infusion of powerful keyboardist Joe Jackson, and as a result of Baker's remix, 'Left of Center' morphed into a rip-roaring rocker and fit in well with other quickly-moving selects in the John Hughes American teenage film, *Pretty in Pink*. In fact, Addabbo conjured up his own creative version of his co-written song for his 2022 studio album.

Related Tracks
'Black Widow Station'
This ballad was written in the form of a traditional Delta blues song, with a casual, conversational tone and repetitive phrases.

Suzanne Vega: Sessions at West 54th
Recorded: 16 June 1997
Released: 1997 (Japan), 1998 (US)
Label: A&M
Running time: 24:44
'Marlene on the Wall' (Vega), 'Gypsy' (Vega), 'Caramel' (Vega), 'Small Blue Thing' (Vega), 'World Before Columbus' (Vega), 'Luka' (Vega), 'Cracking' (Vega)

Live at the Stephen Talkhouse
Personnel:
Suzanne Vega: guitar, vocals
Billy Masters: guitar
Mike Visceglia: bass
Doug Yowell: drums
Recorded: 29 August 2003, Amagansett, New York
Released: 25 October 2005
Label: United Musicians
Running time: 57:14
'Tired of Sleeping', 'Widow's Walk', 'Caramel', 'Marlene on the Wall', '(I'll Never Be) Your Maggie May', 'Penitent', 'Gypsy', 'Left of Centre', 'Harbor Song', 'Queen and the Soldier', 'Blood Makes Noise', 'Luka', 'Tom's Diner', 'Rosemary'

Solitude Standing: Live at the Barbican
Recorded: 16 October 2012, London Barbican
Released: 18 February 2013
Label: Concert Live Ltd.
Personnel:
Suzanne Vega: acoustic guitar and vocals
Gerry Leonard: guitar

Mike Visceglia: bass
Doug Yowell: drums
Alison Balsom: trumpet
Hazel Fernandez: backing vocals

Disc One:
'Tom's Diner' (Vega), 'Luka' (Vega), 'Ironbound/Fancy Poultry' (Vega), 'Solitude Standing' (Vega), 'Calypso' (Vega), 'Language' (Vega), 'Gypsy' (Vega), 'Wooden Horse/Caspar Hauser's Song' (Vega)

Disc Two:
'Marlene on the Wall' (Vega), 'Left of Centre' (Vega), 'Tombstone' (Vega), 'Blood Makes Noise' (Vega), 'The Queen and the Soldier' (Vega), 'Some Journey' (Vega), 'Tom's Diner (Reprise)' (Vega), 'Caramel' (Vega), 'In Liverpool' (Vega), 'Rosemary' (Vega)

Live at the Speakeasy
Recorded: 17 April 1985, Speakeasy, New York
Released: 20 October 2014
Label: All Access
Thirteen tracks drawn from multiple albums plus a brief introduction.

Live at the Bottom Line, NY 1986
Released: 20 April 2020
Label: Air Cuts

Live at Warfield Theatre, San Francisco, 6 August 1987
Both Sets (Remastered), Live FM Radio Broadcast (Remastered)
Released: 18 May 2015
Length: 1:16:01
Label: BKC (2)

Eighteen songs and a 30-second introduction. The backing band included: drummer Steve Ferrara, keyboardist Anton Sanko, lead guitarist Mark Schulman, bassist/vocalist Michael Visceglia and Suzanne Vega on lead vocals and guitar. According to *wolfgangs.com*, an excerpt from the liner notes reads: 'She is in prime musical form on this recording...' and 'She is boosted by a backing band that allows her to shine, both vocally and as a stage performer.'

An Evening of New York Songs and Stories
Released: 11 September 2020
Venue: Café Carlyle
Label: Amanuensis, Cooking Vinyl

Highest Chart Rank: US Current: 70
Running time: 1:02:23
UK: Did not chart or not released in that specific area, US: 70

The album was recorded live at the legendary Café Carlyle, which opened in 1955. The cabaret-style room has featured Bobby Short, Eartha Kitt and Judy Collins, among others. Café Carlyle is one of New York City's most elegant and intimate venues. Patrons are expected to observe a dress code and leave loud conversations outside the door.

For her premiere, Vega performed alongside guitarist Gerry Leonard, bassist Jeff Allen and keyboardist Jamie Edwards. Cooking Vinyl CEO Marvin Goldschmidt explained that 'Suzanne arranged it all herself without our (Cooking Vinyl's) involvement,' and stressed that the label was 'not involved until afterwards. Suzanne decided and organized it all.'

Part of Vega's appeal was the casual and often humorous banter that preceded her songs. She included salutations and brief backstories. For the article published on 14 January 2021, 'Suzanne Vega Doesn't Mind Explaining Her 'Weird' Songs, As Long As You Applaud Afterwards,' *allmusic.com* journalist C. Steffen asked Vega about her decision to explain the content of her songs, or a little bit about the backstories when performing live, as this hadn't been her modus operandi in earlier years. Vega replied:

I tell people what the songs are about because I honestly think you probably wouldn't know what they were about unless I tell you. The shows that I've done where I don't speak, it quickly becomes weird.

Vega has confided in interviews that her more abstract songs, such as 'Cracking' or 'Small Blue Thing' could be misunderstood because, when writing, she focused on the process and was not preoccupied with audience reception. That said, part of the allure can be attributed to her use of informational commentary, whereby the listener feels included in Vega's creative, and at times, idiosyncratic universe.

On his website, Gerry Leonard relayed that he used a 'mobile recording unit and recorded to multi-track' to capture the concert songs and Vega's commentary. Recording acoustic and electric instruments, along with vocals, asides and crowd murmurs, can be a technological challenge, but Leonard and his team knew their stuff. Leonard:

When we played the Café Carlyle in 2019, it was our second time playing that room. We learned a few things from the last time. Suzanne knew that she wanted a strong theme for the evening, a special show. She decided on the theme of New York songs and stories.

I knew I needed to design a show that would suit the room and the idea of a classic piano, upright bass and guitar, but with the twist of adding some vintage keyboard elements and my own textured guitar to give it a modern sound.

Once we got everything worked out the first week, the new challenge was to bring in a small-footprint digital recording system and try to capture Suzanne, the band and the atmosphere of the club. We found an excellent recording engineer in Fernando Lodeiro, who figured out a discreet way to capture three nights of performances.

I spent weeks with the hard drives compiling the best performances, and Suzanne helped me pick and edit the best stories. Kevin Killen brought his magic to mix the recordings, not without the challenge that, with all the instruments so close together, it was hard to get separation; for instance, the upright bass was right behind the grand piano. In the end, Kevin made it work and we got the wonderful album finished.

'Marlene on the Wall' (Vega), 'Luka' (Vega), Conversation: 'So how many people are here from out of town?', 'New York Is A Woman' (Vega), Conversation: 'This next song takes place on 59th Street…', 'Frank and Ava' (Vega), Conversation: 'So, I came to New York City when I was 2 ½ years old', 'Gypsy' (Vega), 'Freeze Tag' (Vega), 'Pornographer's Dream' (Vega), Conversation: 'This next song is called New York Is My Destination', 'New York Is My Destination' (Vega), Conversation: 'The First Time I Saw Lou Reed,' 'Walk on the Wild Side' (Vega), 'Ludlow Street' (Vega), 'Cracking' (Vega), Conversation: 'And Now We've Got a Song About Those Times', 'Some Journey' (Vega), Conversation: 'I'm Gonna Close With This Song,' 'Tom's Diner' (Vega), Conversation: 'Would You Like Another One?', 'Anniversary' (Vega), 'Tombstone' (Vega), 'Thin Man' (Vega)

Acoustic Albums

Close-Up Series
Released: 12 August 2014
Label: Amanuensis
This CD box set contains acoustic albums from 2010-2012, bonus tracks and a DVD performance.

Leonard:

> Suzanne had the idea to record all her songs almost as she would have originally written them, just acoustic guitar and voice. It was really wonderful to hear the songs this way. As we progressed through this ambitious project, it seemed to make sense for the pallet to expand into incorporating some of the arrangements we had used in our duo shows. And then, as we went further, it felt appropriate to add some other colors, like mandolin, harmonium and piano, but keep it very much in the acoustic realm. Each song presented itself in its own way but it was nice to have this wide pallet to choose from.

Close-Up Vol. 1, Love Songs (Suzanne Vega)
Released: 2 February 2010
Label: Amanuensis/Cooking Vinyl
Highest chart rank: UK: Did not chart, US: Did not chart

Close-Up Vol. 2, People & Places (Suzanne Vega)
Released: 12 October 2010
Label: Amanuensis/Cooking Vinyl
Highest chart rank: UK: Did not chart or was not released in that specific area, US Folk: 10, US Current: 186

This year, Vega released the first two albums of this four-part series of stripped-down, re-recorded songs that focused on her original melodies and lyrics from 1985-2007 with intentionally spare accompaniment. Vega had no access to the original masters after being dropped by Blue Note but owned her own material, so she elected to take a fresh look at her classic songs.

The project prompted mixed fan reviews: some, who already owned the records, felt less inclined to duplicate what they already had. But others took a chance, loved the return to Vega's lesser-produced days and took a deeper dive into lyrics they'd forgotten.

Close-Up Vol. 3, States of Being (Suzanne Vega)
Released: 11 July 2011
Label: Amanuensis/Cooking Vinyl
Highest chart rank: UK: US: Did not chart or not released in that specific area

Vega followed up the first two of the series with this album. Here the fans get a sneak preview of her Carson McCullers's tribute with 'Instant of the Hour After', a co-write with Duncan Sheik.

The focus here is on mental health in all its incarnations. Guitarist Leonard's electric dynamics go full-speed ahead on several of the tracks; for example, in 'Blood Makes Noise', his distortion momentarily makes you forget this was a theoretical back-to-basics project, and a lovely violin solo graces 'Fifty-Fifty Chance'. Needless to say, Vol. 1 and 2 were predictably more skeletal, but who says less is always more?

Close-Up Vol. 4, Songs of Family (Suzanne Vega)
Released: 21 September 2012
Label: Amanuensis/Cooking Vinyl
Highest chart rank: UK: US: Did not chart or not released in that specific area, BEL (FL): 160

Vega had written 'The Silver Lady' and 'Brother Mine' over 30 years earlier but the two songs had not been heard prior to this 2012 release. She worked with multi-instrumentalist Gerry Leonard to create a series of demos that would lead the team to produce *Tales from the Realm of the Queen of Pentacles* in February 2014.

Guest Spots

Dark Night of the Soul
Released: 12 July, 2010
Label: Parlophone (Europe), Capitol (North America)
Highest chart rank: UK Albums (OCC): 32
US Billboard 200: 24, US Top Alternative Albums (Billboard): 5, US Top Rock
Albums: 9
Running time: 46:18
Producers: Danger Mouse and Sparklehorse

This studio album featured collaborations with musicians who also assisted with composition and production. Clocking in at 3:09, Vega delivered an appropriate emo lead and backing vocals on 'The Man Who Played God', accompanied on organ, synthesizer, acoustic and electric guitar by Brian 'Danger Mouse' Burton and Mark 'Sparklehorse' Linkous.

On 9 June 2009, Andy Pareti of *Slant Magazine*, wrote: "The Man Who Played God' does not ascend above the kind of stale alt-folk we've heard from many a '90s college-rock band' but does not comment specifically on Vega's vocals.

The project also included, among others, Julian Casablancas (The Strokes), Black Francis (The Pixies), Iggy Pop and David Lynch. *The New York Times* gave the album 'mixed reviews' while *The Guardian* awarded the record four stars.

Deadicated: A Tribute to The Grateful Dead
also featured a collaboration with various artists.
Released: 23 April 1991
Label: Arista
Running time: 74:33

Although this tribute album entailed a hodge-podge of producers, Vega's tracks were exclusively master minded by executive producer Ralph Sall.

As part of the star-studded, massive line-up, which included Los Lobos, Elvis Costello, Indigo Girls, Dr. John, Dwight Yoakam and Jane's Addiction, Vega was the sole artist selected to sing on multiple tracks: 'Cassidy' (John Weir, John Perry Barlow) and 'China Doll' (Jerry Garcia and Robert Hunter). Her backing band includes familiar faces: Marc Schulman on guitar and tiple, Anton Sanko on pump organ and Akai S-1000 and bassist Michael Visceglia.

Vega performed at Madison Square Garden with the Grateful Dead in 1988 at a rainforest benefit. On a YouTube video ten years later, Vega performed these classics with guitarist Gerry Leonard and exclaimed: 'I think of Jerry Garcia very fondly when I do them.'

DNA Taste This featuring Suzanne Vega (1992)
UK: 2, US: 5, AUT: 1, IRE: 2

Remember that Vega's 'Tom's Diner' became a breakthrough dance hit when DNA partnered with the 'Tom's Diner' tunesmith and that fans ultimately got the best of both worlds. Lesser known, is Vega's sensuous rendition of her original 'Salt Water'. This heavily percussive, underrated gem is stitched together with stabs of synth, a spoken-word tease and an instrumental string line reminiscent of James Bond 1964 film theme, 'Goldfinger'.

Tower of Song: The Songs of Leonard Cohen
Released: 1 January 1995
Label: A&M

Thirteen artists, including Tori Amos, Don Henley, Trisha Yearwood, Elton John, Peter Gabriel, Willie Nelson and Billy Joel, paid tribute to the Canadian poet/musician.

Vega enhanced her soulful version of 'Story of Isaac' with a Spanish-style guitar accompaniment and exceeded expectations with heartfelt vocals. Ron Sexsmith's riveting electric guitar and Jerry Marotta's bare-boned but striking percussion added an additional layer of depth. Producer/keyboardist Mitchell Froom and Tchad Blake also joined forces.

Time and Love, The Music of Laura Nyro
Released: 13 May 1997
Running time: 58:58

Fourteen female musicians commemorated the timeless, original music of the late New York singer-songwriter (who penned songs for The Fifth Dimension, among others) by covering her iconic ballads shortly after her death from ovarian cancer. The album also included American vocalists Phoebe Snow and Roseanne Cash, Canadian Jane Siberry and the UK's Lisa Germano.

In an *allmusic.com* review on 13 May 1997, 'Time and Love: The Music of Laura Nyro Review,' the writer stated:

Suzanne Vega's plainspoken, hush-like vocals provide a wintry feel on 'Buy and Sell'. This dark tale of love, sex and pain, complete with Mitchell Froom's quiet piano accompaniment, allows Vega to present Nyro's lyrical anguish.

Songs from Liquid Days
Released: 31 March 1986
Label: Sony BMG Music Entertainment

Vega co-wrote poetic text for 'Lightning' and 'Freezing' on this imaginative Philip Glass retrospective. Paul Simon, David Byrne and Laurie Anderson were also selected lyricists.

Philip Glass, The Complete Sony Recordings
Released: 14 November 2016.
Label: Sony Classical

Vega's text from 'Lightning' and 'Freezing' reappears in the *Songs from Liquid Days* section in conjunction with Michael Riesman on disc twelve of this colossal 24-disc recording.

Pitchfork critic, Seth Colter Walls, noted a disconnect between the 'harmonic progressions,' 'ensemble tempos' and 'the pop-song lyrics' but concluded: 'Still, it's a fascinating look at a composer with a long corporate leash, and a willingness to play around.'

A Tribute to Jack Hardy
Released: 2016
Label: Smithsonian Folkways Recordings/Smithsonian Records

This two-disc CDR includes 26 tracks. On the first disc, Vega sincerely honors the 2:23 'Saint Clare' using fingerstyle accompaniment. The album includes Village troubadour Lucille Kaplansky.

Compilation Albums
Tried & True: The Best of Suzanne Vega (Suzanne Vega)
Released: 28 September 1998
Highest chart rank: UK: 46, US: NOR: 8
Label: A&M
UK: 45, NOR: 8, BEL (FL): 16

This premiere compilation comprised of material from Vega's first five albums also includes 'Left of Center' which had been previously only found on the *Pretty in Pink* soundtrack. 'Book of Dreams' was the sole track taken from *Days of Open Hand* but tracks from more highly rated albums were highlighted. Both versions of 'Tom's Diner' appear, perhaps to appease both the fans and detractors.

'Book & A Cover' and 'Rosemary (Remember Me)' grant the new or veteran listener a taste of the latest and include a sampling of Vega 'live'. A greatest hits album is always subjective, but this generous seventeen-track celebration of Vega's continued growth as a songwriter is an excellent starting point for novices, and for the fan who bypassed the collection-at-large and chooses to play catch-up. Lamentably, 'My Favorite Plum' did not get picked – excuse the pun – but the rest of the album yielded exactly what was promised.

Singles and Related Tracks:
'Book & a Cover', 'Rosemary (Remember Me)'

Retrospective: The Best of Suzanne Vega
Released: 22 April 2003
Label: A&M
Highest chart rank: UK: 27, Certified Gold

This double-CD compilation includes the short, but brassy 'Woman on the Tier (I'll See You Through)', inspired by the book that led to the screenplay of *Dead Man Walking*. On YouTube, Vega explains that the lyric is based on the words of the nun involved in this prison-based story. Vega incorporated 'metal and people shouting' to create a realistic atmosphere. The 21-track album includes one live track: 'The Queen and the Soldier', and though released in the UK (7 July), Europe (April) and the US the same year, the UK version was labeled a 'Special Edition'.

EP – iTunes Festival: London 2008
Released: 5 August 2008
Label: Outsider Art

Bibliography

Books:

Barone, R., *Music & Revolution: Greenwich Village in the 1960s*, Backbeat Books/Rowman and Littlefield Publishing Group, Lanham, Maryland, 2022.
Davis, S., *The Craft of Lyric Writing*, Writer's Digest Books, Cincinnati, Ohio, 1985.
Kaplan, J., *Frank: The Voice*, Anchor Books, New York and Random House, Canada, 2010.
Robinson, L., *There Goes Gravity, A Life in Rock and Roll*, Riverhead Books, NY, 2014.
Stambler, I., *The Encyclopedia of Pop Rock and Soul*, St. Martin's Press, NY, 1989.
Vega, S., *The Passionate Eye, The Collected Writing of Suzanne Vega*, Harper Collins, May 2001.
Woliver, R., *Hoot! A Twenty-Five Year History of the Greenwich Village Music Scene*, 29 April 2020.
Woodworth, M., Solo: *Women Singer-Songwriters in Their Words*, 10 August 1998.

Interviews with author Lisa Torem:

Addabbo, Steve, 9 June 2022
Anderson, Ian, August 2022
Barone, Richard, 19 October 2022
Goldschmidt, Martin, 7 September 2022
Gordon, Jonathan, 10 June 2022
Kaplansky, Lucille, 29 August 2022
Klose, Jann, 30 May 2022
Leonard, Gerry, 22 January 2023
Sheik, Duncan, 16 September 2022
Shendale, John Philip, 14 June 2023
Vega, Suzanne:
13 March 2016
15 January 2015
19 June 2014
8 November 2012
www.pennyblackmusic.co.uk

Additional Interviews:

Burke, K., *Hometown Virtual Conversation with Suzanne Vega*, 22 June 2021.
Ellen, M., BBC TV *Whistle Test*, 24 June 1986.
Jack Hardy, *www.jackhardy.com*, 2000.
Harper Entertainment, 1999.
Simon, T., Howard Stern interview with Suzanne Vega, YouTube, 1993.
stevepafford.com., 'Suzanne Vega Talks Lou Reed,' 27 October 2020.

Toth, E., 'TVD Radar: The Podcast with Evan Toth,' Episode 45: Suzanne Vega, *thevinyldistrict.com*, 10 September 2021.
Vega, S., Interview with Leonard Cohen, excerpted from *The Passionate Eye: The Collected Writings of Suzanne Vega*.

Podcast/YouTube/TV:
C86 Show: Indie Pop, Re: Gerry Leonard – David Bowie and Suzanne Vega, *c86show.org,* 29 September 2021.
Fresh Air Archive with Terry Gross, Interview with Mitchell Froom (99F), *freshairarchive.org*, 10 November 2016.
How a Great Song Helped Change the Way We Listen to Music, 21 January 2020.
The Factory: 1987, Australia.
The Late Show: BBC 2-1, 1993, Re: *Blood Makes Noise, youtube.com*, February 1993.
Tucker, K., The Howard Stern Interview, *ew.com*, 22 January 1993.
Cook, S., CNN, Australia, youtube.com.

Articles:
Blangger, T. and *The Morning Call*, 'L.V. Performers Land Slot for NYC Folk Club Celebration Entertainment,' www.mccall.com, 13 September 1985.
Boilen, B., 'How Lenny Kaye, The Godfather of Garage Rock, Illuminated 'The Psalms,' *npr.org,* 24 March 2017.
Browne, D., 'How Bob Dylan's Rolling Thunder Revue Paves the Way for the Eighties Folk Revival,' *Rolling Stone,* 20 June 2019.
Chiu, D., '30 Years Ago: 'Solitude Standing' Propels Suzanne Vega to Stardom,' *diffuser.fm*, 1 April 2017.
Christgau, R., *Consumer Guide Reviews, Village Voice*, 30 July 1985.
Classic Pop, 'Vive La Vega – Suzanne Vega Interview,' 12 July 2017.
Cook, R., 'Suzanne Vega, a leading figure of folk music revival to appear at The Apex,' *news.suffolkvillage.info.*, 2019.
Dunbar, D., 'Musician Suzanne Vega on the Pandemic, Songwriting and her Upcoming Tour,' *alextimes.com, 2 September* 2021.
Harrington, R., *Washington Post*, Suzanne Vega Review, 6 November 1985.
Holden, S., 'The Times They Are A-Changin',' *New York Times*, 3 September 1985.
Holden, S., 'Bill Morrissey, Blue-Collar Angst with a Folk Touch,' *New York Times,* 23 February 1992.
Hopper, J., Geffen, S., Pelly, J., 'Building a Mystery: An Oral History of Lilith Fair,' *Vanity Fair*, 30 September 2019.
Krein, K., 'Duncan Sheik Continues His Efforts to Merge Electronic & Acoustic Worlds on Claptrap; His First Pop Record in Seven Years, *atwoodmagazine.com*, 5 September 2022.
Lowe, Z., 'Adele: The '30' Interview,' *Apple Music*, YouTube, November 2021.

Moser, J., *blogs.mccall.com*, 16 November 2011.

NY Times, 'Folk City Ends 25-Year West Village Stand,' 28 March 1986.

Pilato, G., 'A Question of Time-An Interview with Gerry Leonard,' *bluebirdreviews.com*, 24 March 2019.

The Observer, *The Guardian*, 'Women on Bob Dylan,' 16 October 2016.

Portwood, J., 'Suzanne Vega on Carson McCullers, Gender, Identity, Britney Spears,' *Rolling Stone*, 12 October 2016.

Ruhlman, W., Suzanne Vega Review, (Re: 1985 self-titled debut), May 2022, *allmusic.com*.

Sandow, G., *rw.com*, 20 April 1990.

Spevak, J., 'Lucy Kaplansky's Songs Tell of Her Journey,' *democratsandchronicle.com*, 21 September 2013.

Stagoff, C., 'Suzanne Vega Will Livestream New York Songs from Powerful New Album to the World,' *njarts.com*, 2 October 2020.

Steffen, C., 'Suzanne Vega Doesn't Mind Explaining Her 'Weird' Songs, As Long as You Applaud Afterwards,' *allmusic.com*, 14 January 2021.

Steinberg, R., 'Man in the Mooncusser,' Interview with Christopher Seufert, newenglandfilm.com, 1 September 2003.

thetimes.co.uk., 'Lou Reed Changed My Life – Artistically and Actually,' 2 November 2013.

Walls, S.C., 'Philip Glass, The Complete Sony Recordings,' *Pitchfork*, 14 November 2016.

Willman, C., 'Queen of Solitude,' *www.latimes.com*, 26 July 1987.

Websites:

digitalcollections.barnard.edu
gerryleonardspookyghost.com
Jackhardy.com
www.pennyblackmusic.co.uk.
suzannevega.com
undertheradar.com
villagepreservation.com